Lynched

A Conservative's Life on a New York City School Board

Frank Borzellieri

Cultural Studies Press

Copyright © 2009 Cultural Studies Press

All rights reserved, including the right to reproduce this book or parts thereof.

First Printing

Cultural Studies Press
New York, New York

www.culturalstudiespress.com

Additional copies of this book may be ordered directly from the publisher.

Library of Congress Control Number: 2008909865

Borzellieri, Frank.
      Lynched: a conservative's life on a new york city school board /
      Frank Borzellieri, Herbert London.
      New York, NY : Cultural Studies Press, 2009.
      p. cm.

ISBN 9780981540719

Cover photograph by Laureen Longo.

Manufactured in the United States of America.

*Dedicated to
Art Beroff*

"*A friend loveth at all times, and a brother is born for adversity.*" *(Prov. 17: 17).*

Contents

Acknowledgments	1
Foreword	2
Introduction	4
1 The Myth of District 24	9
2 My Battle Against Multiculturalism	16
3 American Cultural Superiority	70
4 Banning Pro-American Books	81
5 The Bilingual Follies	100
6 Reckless Liberal Spending	121
7 Homosexual Encroachment	128
8 Victory on Election Day	165
Afterword	174
Rogues Gallery of Liberals	176
Print Media Sources	179
Index	186
About the Author	193

Multicultural Madness

This multicultural book above was the type of book you would find everywhere in District 24. But the wonderful classic below, "Paul Revere's Ride," was banned by the school board from the district.

Banned!

Lynched

A Conservative's Life on a New York City School Board

Acknowledgments

I can say quite accurately that this book was more than a decade in the making. The amount of material that needed to be mined was daunting, to say the least. Piles of press clippings, school board meeting minutes, hours of audio tapes of board meetings and radio shows, and hours of television talk shows and news reports were pored over meticulously, and I could not possibly have done it all myself.

Special thanks to Susan LaRussa and Amelia Gilardino for the painstaking efforts in going through all this material with me, and for all the hours they put in on their own time.

I also to want to thank Steve Webster and Alan Krawitz for their promotional expertise.

The advice of Jared Taylor is always needed and appreciated. I must also thank Howard Hurwitz, my fellow columnist at the Leader Observer and the chairman of the Family Defense Council, who was always imparting valuable advice before I could even ask. And special thanks to Jim Lubinskas.

Thanks to Herb London, my very close friend for so many years, who wrote the foreword to this book. Herb is a true champion of the conservative cause. And thanks to my agent, Alex DelPiero, and the editors at Cultural Studies Press.

Finally, I want to thank Art Beroff, the person to whom this book is dedicated, who was taken from us much too soon, and Art's widow Carol. Art was a Democrat on a different school board in Queens, a man with the most moderate sensibilities and politics, whose reactions to my activities on the school board were always first and foremost to laugh. He was one of the best and closest friends I ever had, and his friendship was something I will always remember with the greatest affection.

Foreword

By Herbert London

If one wants to understand the wayward dimensions of school board activity in New York, there is no better way than to read the following pages in this book. In my opinion, Frank Borzellieri has provided a careful analysis of the left-leaning agenda that has insinuated itself into the New York City school curriculum to the detriment of students and the welfare of the nation.

As a fellow conservative living and working in New York City, I have a full appreciation of what Frank was made to endure from the very liberal political establishment here in this city. While the pages of this book are filled with incidents which were national news at the time they occurred, the immediate and up-close hostility Frank encountered was the result of his daring to be a conservative in a city dominated by liberals.

The New York City political and educational establishments are so far to the left that it was obvious that they simply did not know how to cope with an articulate conservative within their midst. Hence, rather than debate Frank Borzellieri on the merits of the issues, they set about to besmirch him as a person – a certain sign that they knew they had really lost the argument.

The elitists responsible for this condition are driven by deep seated ideological impulses. As a school board member, Frank Borzellieri attempted to forestall the revolutionaries at the barricade by asking poignant questions and challenging their assumptions. It wasn't easy and Frank wasn't always successful.

In addition, even presumptive allies, in a desire for public attention, acceded to the will of the education revolutionaries. Frank remained steadfast. For that and so many other contributions he deserves the acclaim of New Yorkers. But like so many stalwart souls, his achievements have been greeted with silence, or worse, condemnation.

One of the things that extreme liberalism revealed about itself during Frank Borzellieri's eleven year saga as an elected school board member, is that the left is simply not used to any opposition whatsoever in New York. They betrayed a great sense of insecurity about even tolerating a dissenting voice.

Whether it was the multicultural fanatics who would undermine American institutions, radical bilingualists, the extreme homosexual movement which has been successful in infiltrating school curriculum, or the reckless spenders, Frank Borzellieri's detractors demonstrated that they certainly believed, in Frank's own words, "one voice of dissent is one too many."

Yet, as this book indicates, Frank is a genuine hero in the school wars who in my humble opinion will be remembered by those who still believe in the essential righteousness of the American idea and who believe as well that we have a responsibility to transmit to the young an appreciation of our national traditions.

Introduction

My entire eleven years on a New York City school board, District 24 in Queens, was one long battle against the brutal unforgiving forces of political correctness. So when I was deciding with my editors what exactly should be included in this book, we easily arrived at the consensus. Since this book is the documentation of my personal travail in fighting the liberal forces on the school board and the political establishment, I do not analyze in these pages every minute detail of the disastrous educational programs implemented in America's public schools. This book is not about the overall catastrophe of the public schools per se. Certainly, since I'm documenting the activities of a school board, many disastrous programs will be mentioned, especially as they apply to District 24, but for a comprehensive analysis of America's public schools, I recommend starting with the works of Thomas Sowell and going from there.

Likewise, this book's purpose is not so much to focus on the anti-academic and immoral behavior and corruption of too many education insiders, although some of that is revealed, too. Rather, it is my intention to show in the subsequent chapters of this book just exactly how I, as a conservative – an outspoken, committed, true-believing conservative – was treated on a New York City school board by the education and political establishments.

In addition to examining my treatment at the hands of liberal school board members and education insiders, I will also document my confrontations with Ed Koch, Geraldo Rivera, the New York Times and other media. Moreover, the reactions to my school board activities of then-New York City Mayor Rudy Giuliani and other public officials will shed light on the near-monolithic view of a liberal political establishment – where liberals can speak their minds when attacking me, but so-called conservatives are forced to hide like frightened puppies when faced with the prospect of defending someone who tells the truth about cultural or racial issues.

You may want to first tip a glance at the section in the back of

Introduction 5

this book, the Rogues Gallery of Liberals (pages 176-178), in order to familiarize yourself with the various left-wing oddballs mentioned throughout this book. This Rogues Gallery includes school board members and their voting records, listing the percentage of their votes that were liberal. As you can imagine, the most common numbers are 100 and 99 percent liberal. The Rogues Gallery also lists other public players who figured prominently (in a negative sense) in the controversies documented herein.

As conservatives in the academic world understand, conservatives' motives are always assumed to be informed by bigotry and hatred and are otherwise reactionary, while the motives of liberals are always assumed to be honorable. When I criticized the Martin Luther King holiday and objected to a children's book which portrayed King as a virtual saint (while a book on Columbus depicted the explorer as a madman), my detractors never bothered to debate me on the specific issues I raised, namely King's communist affiliations, plagiarism, and so forth. Rather, they used the tactic they always use: accusations of racism. Indeed, both then and now, accusations of bigotry, as they say, are the last refuge of a scoundrel.

In documenting all of this, I should say something about how this book is written. This book is probably the most thoroughly sourced book in history. For many incidents described herein, there are the usual newspaper and magazine references listed in the source section in the back. But in addition to print media sources, I also utilized video and audio tapes of all the television and radio programs and news reports I reference. And still on top of that, I used the minutes of school board meetings, as well as the audio recording of the meetings, and of course, my own ears, since I was there. So for every incident I describe and quote, there are often two, three or four overlapping sources. I also utilized typed transcripts created from audio recordings of board meetings. The transcripts were typed up either by school board staff or by private companies commissioned and paid by me. When I refer to private conversations, I am not merely going from my memory (which is close to photographic, by the way) but from the notes I deliberately took at the time.

On the handful of occasions when I allude to my *personal* "sources," it should be no surprise that I had a few secret friends in the district who would feed me information. In my eleven years on the board, I also dated two divorced mothers and three teachers who occasionally told me things. Whatever the value of the information these girls gave me, it always turned out to be accurate.

The tabulations for the liberal voting records were computed excluding routine procedural votes such as accepting minutes, voting to approve the dates of special meetings, etc. The voting percentages used only those votes which were of a distinct ideological bent, where it can easily be determined whether a vote was "liberal" or "conservative" (such as a vote to approve funding for bilingual education) or procedural votes only if they were deliberate attempts to thwart me.

This book is also not written entirely in chronological order. It is divided by chapters on specific issues (multiculturalism, bilingualism, homosexual influence, etc.) The chapters are generally chronological *within* themselves, but writing the book the way I did, with each chapter concerning a particular issue, was simply the easier way for readers to follow things.

I point this out because I was elected to three terms on the board, from 1993 to 2004. In that time, many different board members were elected, defeated, or retired. In addition, some names will come up who were not yet board members, but were later on the board during other controversies. And you will notice some names appearing, then disappearing. For example, Mary Cummins was on the board for only my first term, so she was prominent in one part of the battle against the homosexual radicals, but was long retired during another part of that battle a few years later. In addition, only board members who were impactful during a particular controversy are mentioned. Board members who were low profile and joined the board in later years are not mentioned at all. (I hope they don't feel left out.) I also refer at various points to different New York City schools chancellors. There were four during my eleven years.

Nevertheless, the flow of the book is effective because for the most part the chronology of events is reported intact, with the

Introduction 7

exceptions I just mentioned.

There are also some interesting things left out of the book because they simply don't conform to the book's major purpose. For example, there is a long story about my fight to enact the district's new Megan's Law policy. As everyone knows, Megan's Law is about protecting young children from child predators. I'm proud that I was the author and sponsor of the new policy. J.D. LaRock, the spokesman for school s chancellor Rudy Crew, told me that my new policy was the impetus for the entire city enacting a newer, tougher policy. He also told me that Crew would never admit it because he didn't want to give me the credit. But because there was no opposition in the district, this is the only mention of the Megan's Law fight (which Crew initially opposed) in this book.

On the school board, being a vocal conservative was tantamount to taking my life into my hands. The objective of my liberal enemies was not only to silence me, but to destroy my career. When speaking in front of normal average citizens at venues other than school board meetings, I often commented that the reason liberals were obsessed with silencing me was not because my ideas were so dangerous, but because they were afraid those ideas would catch on. And so it is true, when I state that bilingual education is a disaster and immigrant children should be forced to learn English, the profound fear my critics have is that such a notion is immensely popular. They are not afraid people will be turned off; they are afraid people are listening.

In the hundreds of letters I received after my battle against multiculturalism, citizens did not merely express support for my positions. More often than not these letters contained the expression, "It's about time!" This was an acknowledgment that I was merely saying out loud what so many of them think. It was also an acknowledgment of the inherent cowardice of politicians – that it took a school board member to assert that American children should be learning about Washington and Jefferson, not African tribal chiefs. Public figures, many letter writers said, were too afraid to say such things out loud.

You will also notice that the press constantly referred to me as the "archconservative" or "ultraconservative" or "extremely conservative" or "right-wing" board member. You will, of course, go blind looking long and hard for any press references to other board members as "ultraliberal" or "archliberal" or frankly, even plain old "liberal."

Copernicus was accused of heresy for violating the orthodoxies of his time. History has shown that telling the truth will often invite the most vicious and hateful attacks when that truth violates those orthodoxies, today known as political correctness. On a school board in the liberal belly of the multicultural beast, the City of New York, violating orthodoxies can also get you lynched.

The Myth of District 24

The School Board of District 24 in Queens, New York, became the most famous school board in the United States in 1992 when it acquired national prominence for stopping the implementation of a curriculum called "Children of the Rainbow," more commonly known as the "rainbow" curriculum, or simply "rainbow." This curriculum was a moral and educational monstrosity which sought to instruct children as young as six years old about the wonders of the homosexual lifestyle. Animated children's books entitled, "Heather Has Two Mommies", "Daddy's Roommate", and "Gloria Goes Gay Pride" became well-known titles in the public consciousness. The chancellor of the New York City public schools, Joseph Fernandez, attempted to use his authority to force Board 24 into accepting the curriculum. At one point, he even suspended the entire board before they were returned to office by the courts. In the end, the district won the battle. New York State law gave authority over curriculum to school boards, and Fernandez's contract as chancellor was not renewed. His ouster was widely attributed to losing this battle against District 24.

The spearhead behind Board 24's opposition to "rainbow" was board president Mary Cummins, a grandmother in her 70's who had previously been an obscure member, but who became a famous national figure as the face of District 24's fight against "rainbow." News on District 24's battle was everywhere, including some major features in conservative publications such as Human Events. As District 24 became the focus of national attention, and as the board, especially Cummins, reaped the benefits of this publicity, public support for the actions of the board was so high that the district attained an image as a bright light on the American scene, defending traditional moral values in the face of a liberal establishment gone morally astray and a bullying chancellor.

Several things happened as a result of this controversy. For the first time, people became aware of just how powerful school boards were. New York City school districts were decentralized to an unusual degree and school districts approved budgets of over $100 million. Although elected by the general public, turnout for school board elections was generally very low. They were held in May instead of November and it did not take a lot of votes to get elected. But on the heels of "rainbow," the public was ready to turn out in record numbers for the 1993 election to vote on one of the hottest political issues of the day.

Like everyone else, I was observing all this and was paying attention to school board matters for the first time. As a political writer, I was always interested in educational issues, but usually I concerned myself with the grand scheme of things. I read Thomas Sowell and other conservatives lamenting the sorry state of public education. But it was not before I decided I wanted to make my mark on all this and run for the school board in 1993 that I focused on exactly what was going on in my own district.

District 24 was basking in the glow of its newly won fame, and because of this the board became known as the great defender of middle class values. The press invariably referred to the board as "white", "middle class", and "conservative." The average person undoubtedly had every reason to believe this, for the only knowledge of Board 24 was from what could be read in the newspapers and seen and heard on television and the radio relating to "rainbow." The board's image as a bastion of traditional conservative values was almost universal.

It was also a crock. I soon came to realize that it was the Big Lie. For lack of a more suitable expression, I will call it "The Myth of District 24."

It did not take long after being elected to the board for me to discover that School Board 24 was every bit as extremist liberal, every bit as morally corrupt, and every bit as intellectually and educationally bankrupt as there existed in America. I also quickly found out that this board contained some of the most squalid ultraliberal freaks as could be found anywhere.

After winning by placing a strong third (behind Cummins and John Garkowski, a Catholic priest) out of 24 candidates, I realized I was not only the most conservative member of the board, I was the

The Myth of District 24

only conservative. Those members who were re-elected, managed to do so by focusing on the only "conservative" thing they had ever done: oppose the "rainbow" curriculum. They would never dare reveal to the public their true liberal voting records.

And even this so-called opposition to "rainbow" was in reality very deceiving. Father Garkowski had told me early on, soon after my election, the true story behind "rainbow" and the board's perceived opposition to it. It was plainly clear to me after a very short time on the board that his version was completely accurate. As evidenced by her longtime voting record, Cummins was far from the "conservative" stalwart that the "rainbow" controversy made her appear to be. She was however, Garkowski said, solely responsible for stopping that curriculum. Garkowski himself, although he had a liberal voting record on all other issues, also believed in the moral necessity of stopping "rainbow." He and Cummins had been allies and friends on the board for many years.

Garkowski told me that early on in the controversy, the other board members did indeed want to compromise on the issue and maybe even cave in. He singled out board member Ed Bagley, whom he called "a horse's ass," as someone who wanted to cave. (Bagley was defeated for unrelated reasons in the 1993 election.) The other members, Garkowski said, were also anxious to cave on the issue. Garkowski had to call a private meeting at his rectory to impress upon the board the importance of putting forth a united front. In addition, Garkowski told me Cummins "knew all the skeletons in people's closets" in District 24 and presumably threatened to use them if any board member caved in. Once the controversy exploded onto the public scene, it became politically untenable for any board members to waffle.

So in reality, the opposition to "rainbow" was only sincere, principled and heartfelt with Cummins and Garkowski. Even if I was inclined to be skeptical of Garkowski's version (which I wasn't), I did not need to be around these people very long to know that he was absolutely right.

In retrospect, it seems foolish for anyone to have thought of the school board as "conservative" based on only one issue. After all, many moderates and moderate liberals were also opposed to that outrageous curriculum. I therefore spent many years on the board trying to explain to average citizens, members of the press, and many veterans of the conservative political movement that opposing the "rainbow" curriculum does not automatically make one a conservative (even without knowing Garkowski's story.)

I became successful in this endeavor by simply being myself and allowing the rest of the world to watch the school board oppose me and attack me. No one in his right mind could examine the voting records and public statements and actions of School Board 24 members and even remotely consider them moderates, let alone conservatives.

On every issue (and I mean *every* issue) which is generally considered a contributor to the downfall of our educational system, the District 24 school board voted monolithically to support and enact the extreme liberal policy. Whether on resolutions allocating millions of taxpayer dollars for bilingual and multicultural education, "self esteem" programs, outcome-based education, the promotion of homosexual propaganda, accepting federal funds for the wacky Goals 2000 program, and overall reckless liberal spending, the board was the willing left-wing perpetrator. While the board spent recklessly, I voted against all federal monies for local education as violating the Constitution.

On the issue that originally brought my name to the forefront – opposing anti-American multicultural education and seeking to end taxpayer financing of these materials – the board showed its true colors. Multicultural materials in District 24, which blamed white Europeans for all the ills of the world, were rampant, as were books trashing Columbus. But materials praising Maya Angelou and Malcolm X were everywhere. When I protested this and tried to put a stop to it, not only did every member of the board come out in vocal opposition to me, but so did the entire education and political establishments. At the school board meeting which took place at the height of this multicultural controversy, I needed a police escort to get home. I was subjected to the most vile public comments, and the audience would not allow me to speak, constantly shouting vulgarities and interrupting. The school board members enabled this, and also enabled my physical safety to be threatened and my point of view to be censored. It was, charitably put, a lynching.

So horrific was the treatment given to me as an outspoken conservative, by both the school board and their allies, that those Americans who still believe that the guarantee of free speech exists for all will now have second thoughts. For I learned the cruel lesson that only an outspoken, libertarian, conservative, Eurocentrist could have learned from this board: as far as the liberals were concerned, one voice of dissent was one too many.

District 24 school board meetings, while technically "public" meetings, were in reality attended solely by employees of the system, liberal education insiders, and radical liberal parents whose interests were pushing a leftist agenda and securing employment for themselves. My old friend, the radio host Bob Unger, said PTA stands for "Patsies for the Administration," meaning, of course, that so-called parent leaders were not interested in representing the true interests of their schools, but were concerned with being in bed with the powerful insiders. So when newspapers reported that at school board meetings "parents" opposed me, I was in reality only opposed by those dullards who attended school board meetings, not parents in general. Even the small number of active parents who secretly agreed with me on the issues and in what I was trying to accomplish were brutishly intimidated into silence. Same with some educators, who were likewise intimidated. My opposition was encouraged to, and was brazen in, speaking out against me; my supporters risked their careers if they outwardly voiced support for me.

Week after week, month after month, I tried to restore some sanity to education in District 24, making the case for conservatives, only to be shouted down and constantly interrupted. As I will show in the following chapters, the board used every procedural device to try and thwart me, even when I attempted to add pro-American books to our libraries and classrooms. Funny how the liberals did not consider this censorship. It is only censorship to object to liberal books. Two sets of rules applied, one for liberals and another for me. Board meetings were often dangerous circuses, where I frequently needed police or security escorts out of the building, to my car, and sometimes even all the way home. All of this simply because I was an outspoken conservative.

My attempts to end taxpayer financing of the obscenity known as bilingual education were similarly met with vitriolic hatred which can only be characterized as hysterical. Illiteracy was rampant in the district, as nationwide, but the liberals on the board would not even agree with me on something that would normally be considered non-ideological. Illiteracy was fine as long as we gave all the children "self-esteem."

If all this clearly demonstrates "The Myth of District 24" and shows the preposterousness of the notion of the board as "conservative," there is more. Much more.

The voting records which I referred to in the introduction and which appear in the Rogues Gallery of Liberals in the back of this book, show such an astonishing collection of liberal extremists that the term "liberal" is a gross understatement. Virtually all influential members of the board in my entire eleven years had voting records of 98 percent liberal or higher! Absolutely none had a conservative voting record. A school board comprised of Jesse Jackson, Barney Frank, and Michael Moore couldn't possibly be more liberal if it tried.

Furthermore, Board 24 was littered with typical white liberal hypocrites – those who claimed to believe in the vital importance of racial integration and multiculturalism and diversity, but who totally disengaged themselves and their families from the specter of nonwhites by living in safe, secure, lily-white neighborhoods. "Integration for thee, but not for me."

In my eleven years, therefore, the school board of District 24 was not merely liberal, but hard extremist left-wing. They simply cannot hide from their voting records and public actions and statements. Only the details in the following chapters can reveal this horrible reality more than my summary here.

There was no difference between school board members who were on the board before me during "rainbow," those who were elected the same time as me, or those who came later. Their ultraliberalism was the same – constant, extreme and consistent.

Slowly but surely, I was successful in revealing all this to the press, to activists and writers in the conservative movement, and to the average person in the street. My actions alone forced the truth to come out. And it was my opening battle against multiculturalism that blew the lid off the "Myth of District 24" for the first time.

My Battle Against Multiculturalism

"I wish that I may never think the smiles of the great and powerful a sufficient inducement to turn aside from the straight path of honesty and the convictions of my own mind." – David Ricardo, economist, 1818

When I received a multicultural "Review Draft" on American history from the district office, I realized that I could not wait any longer for an all-out assault on the multicultural trash that was infesting the district. This curriculum guide was so riddled with anti-American lies and revisionist history that I knew my only strategy had to be to go public.

The section that I was to talk about most frequently was on the United States impact on Haiti during the American occupation in the 1920's. Entitled, "Reaction of a Well-Educated, Wealthy Haitian to the American Occupation", this typical passage read: "Although foreign domination is never a good thing, medicine teaches us that painful operations sometimes effect a cure. The American invasion might have been a good thing if, although unjust and even infringing for a time upon our independence, it had been temporary and had led ultimately to the reign of justice and liberty. But such is not the case. The Americans have not even this excuse. They have made themselves the allies of the evil past of oppression and tyranny; they have abolished liberty, justice, independence; they are bad administrators of public funds; they offer a peace of degradation and subjection, shame and dishonor. They push forward like the rising tide; they attack our traditions, our soul. Is it not claimed that they want to change our culture, our religion?

"Even the good that they do turns to our hurt, for instead of teaching us, they do it to prove that we are incapable. They are exploiters. How can they teach us when they have so much to learn themselves?"

Now this passage and others like it are not only rampant

throughout the curriculum guide, they express the multicultural phenomenon in its essence: anti-American, anti-Western, an angry call for reparations for historical grievances by supposedly oppressed minorities against white Europeans, and outright despicable lies about the West.

In the interests of simplification, I frequently refer to two types of multiculturalism. There is every reason – educational, cultural, and moral – to oppose both. The first type is the more "benign" version which, its proponents assert, merely educates children on the wonders of the various cultures of the country of origin of the different races and ethnicities which comprise the children in the public schools. This strain of multiculturalism is a danger not only because in reality it is far from benign, but because it forces on American children and society something which no other self-respecting society in human history has ever allowed. It is a self-inflicted dispossession that maintains as its central tenet that there is no such thing as an American culture.

American culture, the multiculturalists tell us, is really nothing more than an amalgamation of the various cultures which make up American society. We are a nation of different blood and ethnicities, they assert, and are required to focus on every single culture in order to treat everyone fairly and "celebrate diversity." What?

The proper citizenship papers are all that is required to consider oneself an American, I suppose. By focusing on everyone's "ethnic background" and "country of origin" while ignoring the glorious achievements of the most successful and moral culture in human history – the very distinctive American culture – the multiculturalists are certainly achieving their ultimate goal, the internal destruction of America, which makes perfect sense because they detest America and all it stands for.

The second type of multiculturalism is the more overtly reprehensible and outrageous. It is of the Afrocentric category which maintains that democracy originated in Africa, not Greece; Cleopatra was black; Moses was not Jewish; and blacks are the superior "sun" people because of the melanin in their skin, while whites are the inferior "ice" people. Probably the best known proponent of this nonsense is Leonard Jeffries, a professor at the State University of New York, who was commissioned by the left-wing radical Commissioner of Education Thomas Sobol, to sit on a committee overseeing the multicultural curriculum for the public schools. So Jeffries was approving the curriculum guide which I was supposed to implement in the schools in my district!

At public school board meetings prior to examining the guide, I would frequently quote the brilliant Thomas Sowell's views on multiculturalism to the groans of liberal educators in the audience. When I referred to multiculturalism as "basically trash" and criticized the newly released movie "Geronimo" as the politically correct glorification of a murdering savage, I was challenged by an angry teacher who repeated the tired line that because District 24 was comprised of so many different immigrant groups that we had an "obligation" to teach about other cultures. In response, I vowed to make every effort to keep my campaign promise and rid the district of every last remnant of multiculturalism. Thomas Sowell's book, "Inside American Education", eventually became more than a bible for me. It was now a sort of defensive shield or bullet-proof vest I had to carry around to protect myself from liberal assaults.

The curriculum guide was, of course, a virtual monument to hysterical multicultural grievances against the United States and would have been properly labeled "The Politically Correct Guide to Revisionist History." The theme of the guide was so anti-academic and anti-intellectual, and was so obsessed with discussions of the Ku Klux Klan, white racism and the struggles of ethnic minorities in a criminally oppressive society that I could not decide whether the background music while reading the guide should be sad classical music or the theme from "Jaws."

Entire sections of the guide were designed to have students express their feelings on "bigotry and racism", such as "Puerto Rican immigrants also headed to American cities in the 1920s, mostly to New York City, where they faced bigotry and discrimination." Peculiar exercises and instructions were at the end of each section of the guide, such as, "If you were James, how would you have reacted to the foreman telling you that all African-American firemen were losing their jobs?"

The "Harlem Renaissance" received more attention than World War II. A typical "Focus Question" was, "What were the major ideas that led the emerging struggle for racial equality between wars?" Marcus Garvey is quoted without criticism. "We declare that the entire Negro race must be freed from the factory and farm work, which is little better than slavery," he said.

Another "Focus Question" was, "How did Americans from a variety of cultural groups contribute to the Allied victory in World War II?" It came as no surprise that homosexuals were listed as a "cultural group." "It is not possible to identify the specific numbers who served in the various branches of the military – in the 1940s very few made their homosexuality known. To do so would have meant a dishonorable discharge. But the personal testimony of gays and lesbians today about their experiences in World War II gives witness to the fact that they served valiantly in the war's major battles."

Expanding on this theme, the guide quotes a Ted Allenby: "I enlisted in the Marine Corps. This had a good deal to do with my being homosexual. In my teens, I had come to view my homosexuality as bad, a disease. How do you deal with it? You deal with it by trying to prove how rugged you are…I had the constant need to prove how virile I was."

What in the world does this have to do with teaching history and providing a decent education?

The absurd notion of "moral equivalency" regarding the Cold War reared its ugly head in the guide when Soviet atrocities were not even mentioned, but, the guide asserted, "It is clear, however, that the enmity between the two nations had its roots in United States opposition to the Bolshevik revolution in 1917." Likewise, Ho Chi Minh was described as having "won their independence" and an anti-Vietnam War song's lyrics, "I Ain't Marching Anymore", were printed in their entirety.

The supposedly conservative District 24 issued a "Multicultural Philosophy Statement", which was approved by Mary Cummins' hand-picked choice for district superintendent, Joseph Quinn. The statement read in part, "…District 24's educational programs reflect a *broad-based multicultural approach* (emphasis added)... In formulating goals to meet the needs of its diverse student population the district will address a two-fold objective: to create a school environment that fosters understanding and appreciation of diversity in its many forms; to provide children with the academic and social skills necessary to live responsibly in our global society."

The statement continued, "...giving the children the prerequisite skills to become responsible citizens in a global society, District 24 is committed to the development of curriculum and the implementation of instructional programs designed to promote the development of critical thinking and social action skills. Students will have the opportunity to study the impact of all kinds of discrimination on society and consider solutions for its resolution... District 24 will foster a sense of collective responsibility among students and staff for our earth, its environment, and for society at large."

Such nauseating claptrap was attacked head-on by Thomas Sowell in "Inside American Education", when he referred to "the need for preparing young people to participate in the world community", a statement taken from a 1991 report prepared for the New York State commissioner of education. Sowell stated that "...it was echoing a familiar theme in the multicultural literature. Yet neither argument nor evidence was offered to show how the particular things being done as a part of the multicultural agenda would accomplish that purpose, which was itself left vague."

Cummins endorsed the district's nonsensical left-wing statement at a public meeting when she said, "We have a multicultural program in this district that is second to none."

Press Release

Having digested the guide and read the district's ridiculous statement, and having put up with the overwhelming multicultural sentiment and the hostility that goes with it from the district establishment and the other board members, I decided to issue a press release on my intentions. It stated, in part, that I would

My Battle Against Multiculturalism

eliminate materials promoting multiculturalism, which I termed, "a parasitic intrusion of garbage and lies upon the great Eurocentric tradition in American curriculum." The release continued, "I will personally tour the schools searching for this trash they call multiculturalism – like Sherman through the South if I have to – and find every last book in order to rid our district of this nonsense. It is bad enough to have this trash poison the minds of our children, but to do it with taxpayers' dollars is unconscionable." I would not tolerate materials which state "white Europeans are to blame for all the historical troubles of man. I will not allow this or any other form of so-called 'diversity' to continue to see the light of day in District 24... The United States must retain its cultural identity. Spineless politicians and bureaucrats are now catering to every ethnic interest group and are effectively Balkanizing our nation. If I move to Pakistan, will they teach my kids about the wonders of growing up in Ridgewood, Queens? I don't think so."

I faxed the release at about 10:30pm to the major media and expected some response the next day. I did not have to wait that long. At about midnight, my telephone rang while I was asleep. By the time I reached the phone, a message had already been left on the answering machine by Jay Diamond, the leading late-night radio talk show host on WABC. When I tried to return the call, I continuously got busy signals, so I simply turned on the radio.

Jay Diamond was (along with Bob Grant) one of the best talk-show hosts in New York. He was smart, fair, insightful, and conservative. He was reading my press release on the air, praising it to the hilt. "This guy is great," he said about me. "If anyone knows where Frank Borzellieri is, please have him call the show." As I listened, I continued to get a busy signal while trying to call in. While Jay and the callers were supporting my statement and intentions, Linda Sansivieri, the ultra-liberal board member, got through to the show.

"He's bizarre," she told Jay. "He has no right to do this. We have children of many different cultures in our district." Jay and Sansivieri began discussing the logistical aspect of my plan – whether I had the authority to carry out my intentions. But that was really beside the point. Obviously, on a nine-member board I would need five votes. It was the ideological point that was most important. Was this board against multiculturalism or not? "And Mary Cummins is opposed to Frank Borzellieri," Sansivieri said.

Jay seemed stunned. He described Mary as a "friend", although I suspected this friendship was based on Cummins' fame due to the "rainbow" controversy. After she got off the air, Jay described Sansivieri as a "very conservative" woman. If Linda Sansivieri is very conservative, then Joe Stalin was a civil libertarian. But Jay cannot entirely be blamed for grossly mischaracterizing this leftist political hack because his assumption was the same very common mistake that many people made: without knowing her long liberal and leftist associations, he merely attached the "conservative" label to anyone connected to stopping "rainbow."

When I finally got through to the show, I slammed Sansivieri and the liberal board, vowing to continue to go over their heads and directly to the public. But the liberal attack was on.

The next day, the New York Post called and ran a story the following day entitled, "School-board Member: Textbooks that aren't Eurocentric are Trash." Within a few hours, I was back on the air with Jay Diamond, this time during the day as he was substituting for regular host Bob Grant. Before I went on the air, the producer told me that Mary Cummins would be coming on after me to give the counter point of view. I did not much care for the idea of having Cummins rebut me without the opportunity to defend myself, so I suggested to him that I would be happy to share my air time and engage in a public debate with her. He loved the idea and said he would call me back after proposing it to Cummins. He called me back within twenty minutes. Cummins backed down and would not be going on at all.

During these next few days I knew the liberals were gearing up to pounce on me at the next public school board meeting. I realized they would be coming after me, so I enlisted the help of a couple of old friends. I went to the offices of the Congress of Racial Equality and met with Roy Innis, one of the few outspoken black conservatives who has gained the admiration of many by attacking the monolithic point of view of the so-called "black leadership." Roy and I had worked together in a number of high-profile cases in the pro-gun, anti-crime movement. I had also written pro-gun articles for his organization's publication and helped on his campaign for congress. Roy was one of the first to come out against the anti-white diatribes of Leonard Jeffries.

That night we put together a statement which I released to the press and which I was going to bring with me to the school board meeting later that week. Roy's statement read, "Frank Borzellieri dares to address the issue of multiculturalism when others run and hide. He deserves to be commended for showing courage in the face of mean-spirited attacks and for condemning the lies of multiculturalism. I've known Frank Borzellieri since he was a teenager and have worked with him for many years. I know what he his doing on the school board is in the best interests of the children and our nation."

Herbert London, a dean at New York University, has long been a respected voice in academia and in the conservative movement. In 1990, he garnered more votes than any third party candidate since the Civil War, when he ran for governor of New York State on the Conservative Party line. Now, he was once again a candidate for governor as a Republican. Although he had a great deal at stake, Herb did not hesitate in issuing a strong endorsement of my actions. While he would be out of town on the night of the board meeting, he authorized someone to read it for him. It read, "As the dean of the Gallatin Division of New York University for twenty years, as the author of thirteen books and hundreds of articles on education, and as a lifelong activist in the conservative movement as well as the Conservative Party's candidate for governor in 1990, I wish to take this opportunity to express my full support for District 24's curriculum chairman and my good friend, Frank Borzellieri.

"I regret that I am unable to give this statement in person, but I have a prior speaking engagement upstate. I want to express my unequivocal support for Frank Borzellieri, who has been one of the most outstanding conservative activists in New York City over the years. Frank has been an indispensable ally to those of us who have fought for traditional American values in both education and society at large.

"In addition, Frank has shown the courage to address the controversial issues such as multiculturalism and the harm it is inflicting on our nation. I urge all of you who care about the future of our children to support Frank Borzellieri. Thank you."

Armed with these statements and my own ammunition, I went to the board meeting where the liberals, especially Cummins and Sansivieri, were itching for a fight. The week's events were first mentioned when I reiterated my intention to eliminate taxpayer funding of anti-American materials from the schools in our district. I said that I had no intention of backing down and would tour several schools accompanied by the deputy superintendent. I called multiculturalism a "danger to society", quoting a National Review article which had arrived in my mail that week. I even held up the magazine and quoted editor John O'Sullivan who wrote, "Multiculturalism regards assimilation as a form of oppression; its vision is of America as a permanent conversation among different tribes... Multiculturalism is finally an incoherent idea."

When I blasted the bizarre theories of Afrocentrism, a radical black PTA president, Perry Buckley, jumped out of his seat and started rushing to the stage screaming, "You get more ridiculous every month!" (More on Buckley on the next page.) Cummins defended him, asking me, "What have you got against multiculturalism?" I responded, "If you don't know by now, Mary, then I can't help you."

When Sansivieri began jabbering, I laughed out loud while pointing out that such an extreme liberal as she was identified as a "conservative" by Jay Diamond. When I asked her why she failed to correct Jay, she was silent. You see, the rule still applies: liberalism is the ideology which embarrasses those who subscribe to it, so while they behave like liberals, they understand the benefits of not being so labeled — no one wants to be *called or thought of* as a liberal. Conservatives, on the other hand, suffer no such inhibitions. It is not an embarrassment to be a conservative. This is all axiomatic in American politics, but is particularly manifest in a white, middle class neighborhood like many parts of District 24. Sansivieri, therefore, is very typical of the board members in that they campaign as "conservatives", but run things as the leftists they are.

Arrested for Murder

Digressing on Perry Buckley: What would the District 24 school board be without one of its members being arrested for murder? After all the controversies we had been through, it only seemed morbidly fitting that of 32 school boards in New York City and thousands in the United States, School Board 24 would produce the country's first school board killer – three years after this multicultural controversy.

Perry Buckley (no relation to William F., Jr.) was the board's second black member and the first black actually elected. While the district was bloated with immigrants, only about five percent was black. Louise Emanuel finished 10th in one election and then was appointed to fill a vacancy, but Buckley was the first to gain his seat at the ballot box.

Before his election – and at the time of the controversy described in this chapter – Buckley, a retired fireman in his mid 40's, was parent association president of PS 14 in the neighborhood of Corona, and was a well-known cub scout leader. He was married with two children, including a teenage son. During my first term, he was active as PTA president and often clashed with me on the multicultural issue. After his arrest for murder, Newsday noted that I was actually the one to raise Buckley's public profile because the media often went to him for the opposing point of view. He was a guest with me on the four-man television debate show, "Street Talk" (which I describe later in this chapter) at the time of this multicultural controversy. Newsday also recalled the incident I just described when Buckley had rushed the stage, bellowing at me, "You get more ridiculous every month!" He also took offense when I made fun of the movie "Geronimo" which glorified the Indian. Buckley's wife was part American Indian.

Still, he was one of those people, despite his extreme liberal record, who had a reputation as a well-intentioned, laid back guy who tried to make peace among quarrelling board members. I'm not sure how much I agreed with that analysis, but I certainly got along with him on a personal level. As a black man, he had the political luxury of telling me that he knew that most whites secretly thought like me, a fact that the white liberals would never admit. His public criticisms of me were also much less vicious and personal than most of the other attacks.

When he was arrested for murder, it came out that Buckley, to the astonishment of everyone, was leading a double life. Police reports indicated he was taking crack, had a white girlfriend to whom he gave some of his wife's jewelry, and had been previously arrested for violence against his wife. While all of this came to light after his high profile public arrest, none of us knew that he had already been arrested for domestic violence when he was on the board.

I was quoted in various news articles stating, "It unnerves me that we had a monster in our midst and we didn't know it."

Buckley killed 30-year-old Iris Faulk in a drug-induced rage, stuffed her body under a pile of clothes in a Boy Scout meeting room in his building, and had the locks changed so the building superintendent could not get in and find the body. The odor of decomposition eventually led to the discovery, and Buckley confessed to the murder while police were questioning him about beating his wife. He eventually plea-bargained to second degree manslaughter, and was sentenced to five to fifteen years.

After the arrest, the black schools chancellor Rudy Crew shocked even liberals by refusing to remove Buckley from the board, although he had removed other board members in the city for much less serious offenses. Everyone knew that Crew wanted to avoid having to replace Buckley with someone aligned with me. Crew had established a precedent whereby any vacancy was filled by the candidate who in the previous election had gotten the next-highest vote total. In this case, the next person in line was James Noviello, a friend and ally of mine, so Crew allowed the vacancy to stand for five months! He merely suspended Buckley rather than officially

My Battle Against Multiculturalism

remove him. Finally, under increasing pressure, Buckley himself resigned from the board from prison. Amidst mounting pressure on Crew to act, he finally filled the position – not with Noviello, but with a sworn liberal enemy of mine. Even the New York Times pointed out the chancellor's hypocrisy.

Back to the meeting, when a conservative black political friend of mine went to the microphone and read Roy Innis' statement, he was jeered mercilessly and later, in the lobby of the school, was called an "oreo" (black on the outside, white on the inside) by another radical PTA person.

A spokesman for Herb London read his statement and Cummins went berserk. "What the hell does Herb London know about multiculturalism?" she asked. Sansivieri told the man, "Electioneering is not allowed at a school board meeting," making the ridiculous implication that somehow Herb was using this meeting as a forum to campaign.

The next morning Cummins called Herb at his office, screaming at him and threatening to "destroy" Herb with the Conservative Party in his gubernatorial campaign. (This is a humorous side issue. Cummins, because of all the publicity she received during "rainbow", always tried to give the impression that she was some sort of kingmaker with the New York Conservative Party. Several months later, Cummins sent out a letter to all enrolled Conservative voters in the district in order to discredit me with them. Not only did these voters ignore Cummins, many of them called me, angrily wanting to know if Cummins had lost her mind. Of course she hadn't. She was simply not a conservative and now had egg all over her face by having exposed her true colors to people who might have previously admired her.)

The fallout from the tumultuous week was that although I made my mark on the public scene and left no doubts or ambiguity about my determination and sincerity regarding the elimination of multicultural materials, I also got a glimpse of exactly what kind of vicious fury was awaiting me if I continued on my mission. Little did I know at this time that the attacks on me during the week would prove to be relatively minor compared to what awaited me soon after. Within a week after the meeting, the chairman of the district's PTA's (Patsies for the Administration), Kathy Masi, sent a letter to Mary Crowley, the president of the board, requesting my removal as chairman of the curriculum committee. Masi, the head Patsie, never functioned as a true parent leader, but more as a loathsome shill for the left-wing administration of the district. (Within a year of this incident, she would replace Cummins on the board after Cummins' retirement.) Her letter stated, in part, "After Mr. Borzellieri's most recent display of bad manners, I feel compelled to write you at this time… Mr. Borzellieri obviously does not have any idea what his responsibilities are as the Chairman of the Curriculum Committee and/or as an elected official. It is my opinion that he has consistently wasted our time using his position as a School Board member to promote his own political agenda and beliefs… Mr. Borzellieri's lack of respect during the subject of multiculturalism is a disgrace… Mr. Borzellieri's constant derogatory statements are laced with undertones of hate. These kinds of statements stir our youth and are of an inflammatory nature and if unrestrained will eventually lead to mayhem."

I wanted to respond immediately, but first I had to stop laughing. It is a liberal axiom, of course, that when one pursues a conservative agenda, one is assumed to be treacherous, "promoting a political agenda" and "wasting time." When one pursues a liberal agenda, one is assumed to be honorable, with good intentions and the best interests of the children and society. Setting aside the obvious silliness of the letter, I could rightfully claim a strong conservative mandate from the voters. In a field of 24 candidates, I placed third as a virtual unknown. I ran as an unabashed conservative, so the voters knew my views when they elected me. Even the only two candidates to place ahead of me, Cummins and John Garkowski, although not true conservatives, were *perceived* as conservatives by the voters.

Crowley responded to Masi in a letter stating that I had a right to my opinion and, "Since Mr. Borzellieri has not violated any polices of Community School Board 24 I find that this [removal as chairman of the curriculum committee] is not necessary at this time." This "right to my opinion" turned out to be a right which Crowley would not be respecting much longer.

The week's events also led to a hysterical column by New York Daily News writer Luis H. Francia, who decried my actions as "no doubt taking his cue from Savonarola, the medieval Italian cleric with a penchant for burning books" and called my plan "ethnic cleansing as applied to ideas and should be condemned unequivocally." Events also led to a full-page "Closeup" of me in New York Newsday, one of the city's major dailies, in which the radical black Perry Buckley referred to my "modern-day witch hunt." The article, I was told, was then scotch-taped to a wall in the teachers' lounge in one of the schools by a union leader, as an object of scorn.

As an aside, one of the most common accusations hurled at me throughout my entire time on the school board was that I was "using" my position to promote my own political career. The liberals never understood the contradiction in this. On one hand, they claimed that my ideas were radical and crazy, and no one in his right mind would ever support my agenda. Therefore, by their own logic, I was in the process of *destroying* my career. Of course, secretly, these same liberals knew that outside their little world of liberal education hacks, the overwhelming majority of voters were in agreement with my positions. So in reality, what terrified the liberals was not that they thought I was turning people off. Rather, they were afraid that people were agreeing with me.

This great gulf between the "official" liberal position of the education and political establishments and the views of the general public has always hovered over school board matters, waiting to crash down on the heads of the liberals on the board, particularly the white liberals. For it was these white leftists who embodied the term "limousine liberals," not only by their nutty positions on the issues, but more by their hypocrisy. They not only run as "conservatives" while governing as liberals. They exalt multiculturalism, tell us how wonderful "diversity" is and how we must celebrate it, yet choose to live themselves in lily-white neighborhoods. There was no white liberal board member who lived among other cultures in this ethnically and racially diverse district that they claimed to love so much. They seemed to like only white faces when it came to their own neighborhoods and their own lives. With the exception of Garkowski who, as a priest, had no choice where he lived, they would all be the first to move out if their neighborhood became "darker."

Before the next meeting, I was told that Masi was going around to different schools trying to galvanize opposition to me and enlisting the support of the NAACP. Since one of my secret friends informed me of this, the meeting room was shocked when I responded with full knowledge of the facts. "Do the parents of District 24 know this person, in their name, is aligning herself with a radical, socialist organization like the NAACP? Do they know that she is crawling into bed with an organization that believes in forced busing? With an organization that believes in racial quotas for hiring? With an organization that endorsed... Jesse Jackson for president? Do they know that she is seeking support from an organization that regularly gives aid and comfort to the most vile black street hoodlums in our society. If they do not, rest assured that I will see that they do."

The room sat in stunned silence as I began. As I was finishing, there were screams from the audience. Crowley tried to stop me from completing my statement. I had done the unthinkable – criticized the NAACP. This was the first of several times that I would need a security escort out of the building.

The next step in my protracted quest was to actually begin touring the schools of District 24 and get my hands on what one reporter called "the smoking gun." Much was made by the liberals of the fact that, for all my enthusiasm, I had never actually found anything objectionable in the schools. That was on the order of stating that I had no proof there was sand in the Sahara Desert simply because I had never been there. Besides, I already had that curriculum guide. But in truth, one need not visit a public school to know what exists in its libraries and classrooms, but visit them I did nonetheless.

The Tour

In a tour that would have been properly titled "Journey to the Bottom of the Barrel", I had the district's deputy superintendent arrange for me to visit five of our schools in different neighborhoods throughout the district. We were accompanied by a second district official and two associates of mine with expertise in phonics and reading. One was Bob Unger, an attorney, radio host and author who occasionally gave presentations on the phonics reading method. The other was Charles Richardson, the chairman of a group called Educational Engineering and of another group called the Literacy Council.

Throughout the course of the visits, which lasted the entire day, we observed classes in session, watched a play put on by the children, discussed reading methods with the principals, and walked the hallways which were decorated with various kinds of artwork, essays, decorations and posters. Contrary to the district's public image, the schools indeed were bastions of political correctness guided by multicultural madness. My conversations with some of the principals led me to believe they were merely victims of circumstances against the tide of multicultural dogma, over which they had no control, or had merely acquiesced. Others seemed to embrace multiculturalism and all its baggage wholeheartedly. And there lies one of the most serious problems that I had to endure throughout my entire time on the board. The liberal educators who embrace the system and its anti-academic, anti-intellectual nonsense, are free to speak out. Those who may harbor the belief that I have a legitimate point have been intimidated into silence.

Rather than George Washington, Thomas Jefferson and Benjamin Franklin, the walls of PS 19 in Corona, the district's multicultural heartland, were covered with pictures of Maya Angelou, Bill Clinton's multicultural poet laureate, the black novelist Toni Morrison who said, "At no time have I ever felt as if I were an American", and another leftist from the Clinton administration, Marian Wright Edelman. Also plastered all over the walls were glowing tributes to

Earth Day with accompanying artwork. There were hearts drawn by students for Mother's Day in *Spanish* and a huge politically correct poster entitled "Why Recycle?" Another multicultural monument on a wall was a social studies curriculum collage entitled, "The Nigerian Marketplace." (I wonder if they have the Ridgewood Marketplace in Nigeria.) But what were to eventually cause the volcanic explosion that would forever alter discussion of multiculturalism in the district, and to a great extent, in the entire educational and political establishments in New York City, were my visits to the libraries. It would also forever cement my own public persona as the de facto representative of the anti-multicultural, pro-American point of view. Although I did not realize it at the time, in less than two weeks my life would change forever.

There was a ton of objectionable material in the libraries, most conspicuously those materials promoting multiculturalism and others which simply advanced revisionist history. There was a large children's picture book on Christopher Columbus which depicted the great explorer as a pilferer and madman interested in only spices and riches. No mention was made of his bringing Christianity to the New World or to his efforts at taming an uncivilized continent. On the other hand, the book that would eventually cause the biggest stir, "Young Martin's Promise," a children's biography of Martin Luther King, portrayed King as a virtual saint. It is this type of double standard that permeates the public schools, not to mention society at large. PS 19's library made me feel as if I was in a United Nations conference room without the translating headsets. Books entitled "La Fiesta Del Abecedano", "Haitian Days", "The Sombrero of Luis Luceo", "The Calypso Alphabet" and "The Korean Cinderella" were there.

"I Hate English" was another children's book which was designed to make the American people feel guilty for the fact that we expect immigrants to learn English. PS 68 also had books entitled "Tikki Tikki Tembo" and a book I was to make famous called "Jambo Means Hello: The Swahili Alphabet." Students in District 24 can barely read and write in English, yet taxpayer dollars had to be spent, as a ridiculous sacrifice to the radical multicultural movement, on the Swahili alphabet.

I left the school that day with five of the books in my possession. I sensed a certain nervousness on the part of the principal of PS 19 when I indicated that I would be holding on to the books for awhile. Everyone seemed to feel that I was up to something, although they were not sure exactly what.

Within ten days I met with reporters from Newsday and the New York Post and showed them the "smoking gun" that I had found. Rose Kim of Newsday was a reporter who had covered me extensively for the time that I was on the board. We knew each other quite well and she was anticipating that I would eventually come forward with objectionable material that I would want removed. Although reporting for a very liberal newspaper, her articles were always fair and balanced, and I allowed her to inspect all the books and interview me at length. I felt at this point that I had done my duty as an elected representative of my district. I had made good on my campaign promises and needed to go over the heads of this liberal school board directly to the public. I expected nothing more than the article to appear in the next day's newspaper which would further bring the issue to the forefront of public discussion. When I went to sleep that night, it was the last time in my life that I would be thought of as merely a local figure.

Media Explosion

When I woke in the morning, my name was all over every radio station in the city. The Newsday article hit the stands, the rest of the press picked up on it, and a whirlwind of media frenzy was to become the day.

The first call from a radio station came at 6:30am and the final television camera left my apartment at around 7pm. In between there were ten radio interviews; several more newspapers either called or showed up, and every television station's news cameras were at my home. Entire news crews were waiting outside for their turn. It was the story of the day – not to mention the week – and every major city politician, from Mayor Rudy Giuliani on down, got in on the act.

The Newsday article, which featured a photo of me holding five of the books I wanted removed, was fairly balanced. But it didn't matter. The things I said were simply too politically incorrect for the liberal thought police. The fanatics who wanted to destroy me would never listen to a cogent, well-reasoned explanation.

The article led with what would prove to be the most nerve-shattering aspect of the story — my criticism of the book on Martin Luther King. Now, what I am against is revisionist history in the schools without any sense of balance. To this day, I continue to be labeled as someone who "wants to ban books on Martin Luther King." First of all, books on King as a historical figure are appropriate, just as books on Stalin are appropriate. History is history, whether human figures are objectionable or not. My specific complaint about the King book was that it was on the shelf right beside the book which disparaged Columbus. Now everyone knows that if King had been portrayed negatively (in other words, accurately) the book would have been removed faster than you can say censorship. So my complaint was about gross ideological imbalance. The book portrayed King as a saint. But no issue – not abortion, not social security, not crime – touches a greater nerve, terrifies more people and lights a greater fire under liberal fanatics than the issue of race. And Martin Luther King was black. The fact that my criticisms of King had nothing to do with his race was irrelevant to the establishment. I had, once again, done the unthinkable. Even many sensible people will run for cover at the sound of criticism of Martin Luther King. It has become impossible to engage in a serious, rational discussion about the man, so fanatical and unreasonable are those who idolize him. So when I was quoted as calling him a "leftist hoodlum with significant communist ties" and a "hypocritical adulterer", not one person would debate me on the merits of my argument. And not even one liberal would concede that I had the right to express my opinion.

This mindset of hysterical irrationality manifested itself in my very first radio interview that morning. A puny little twerp named Michael Lebron, who goes by the stage name "Lionel", hosted the morning talk show on the top-rated WABC in New York. (Now he is on the loser liberal Air America.) He was screaming about me before I was even called by the producer to do the show. Lebron is one of those liberal white guys (although he claims to have black and Puerto Rican blood) who sits home at night dreaming up ways to endear himself to the blacks, so as to gain their acceptance. It is an orgasmic experience for him to hurl accusations of racism at people and then say to himself, "Great, now blacks will like me." Lebron is the typical cowardly white person who wants to erect public monuments to himself to prove that he's not a racist. It is truly the most important thing in his life. He badly desires to be named an honorary black. (Of course, he lives in a white neighborhood – far, far away from blacks.) Naturally, I presented him with the opportunity of a lifetime.

As soon as I got on the air, Lebron began asking me about my King remarks. I reminded him that two people with whom I was agreeing the most about King's communist affiliations were two liberal heroes, John and Robert Kennedy. Incredibly, Lebron denied this matter of public record and began shrieking, "You're a racist! You're a racist!" I could barely be heard above his feminine squealing, but I did manage to say more than once, "Why don't you move into this district and run against me?" Like a loser, he responded, "Gee, that's a good one, Frank! You're a racist!" I was making him look so bad that when I asked him if he knew how to read, he cut me off. Now, callers get cut off all the time on radio shows, but this is the first time I ever recall an *invited guest* being cut off, especially when I was the one speaking calmly and the host was the one screaming. As it would turn out, my two biggest on-air supporters that week would come from the same station, Bob Grant and Jay Diamond.

The Martin Luther King issue, which I needed to address time and again, was merely one of political correctness. Today, was can speak publicly about Nixon's warts; we can speak also of JFK's warts and those of LBJ and Reagan. But Martin Luther King is somehow above criticism, no matter how well-documented or well-thought out the arguments.

Although I had always accepted liberal media bias as a fact of life, I thought the bias came into play solely with the angle and reportage of the news. In my experience with the press, no reporter ever exhibited any negative personal feelings while they were dealing with me. This was not the case when veteran Channel 2 television news reporter Reggie Harris came to my home. Although courteous and professional throughout the interview, he was clearly agitated. A tall black man, he was questioning me (before the actual taped on-air interview) not only about the books but about what else I found objectionable in the schools. I mentioned the poster of Toni Morrison and her quote, "At no time in my life have I felt as if I were an American." Harris glared at me with piercing, angry eyes and asked, "Do you know why she said it?" I responded, "I know why, but I have no sympathy for it." Harris then put his notebook on the table, never averting his eyes from me and asking in a lowered voice, "Am *I* an American?" I never actually thought he was going to explode at me, but he later glanced at the Newsday article again and, finally instructing the cameraman to get started, said, "Well, let's finish the story that's upsetting all of us."

Between the phone ringing off the hook all day, and the media in and out, I nearly had no time to breathe. Finally, I would watch some of the television news. And there was the usual cast of liberals calling me the devil incarnate, including spokespeople from the New York Civil Liberties Union and People for the American way, both accusing me of censorship; radical blacks, including the PTA president Perry Buckley; and one woman who said I should be removed from the board and kept away from children. Among the jackals was the mayor of New York City, Rudolph Giuliani, who said, "It sounds pretty outlandish to be challenging a book about Martin Luther King…don't know what the other books involved are, but that seems outlandish and sounds like he has lost his grip on reality."

The Giuliani quote was interesting in that before I was elected, Giuliani was the guest speaker at a party which was thrown for me. He told the crowd how valuable my voice would be, and he certainly was aware of my basic political philosophy when he did this. I had met privately with Rudy on two separate occasions and one of his top aides, Richard Schwartz, who was my contact with the Giuliani team, always told me how highly Rudy thought of me. I could partially accept the fact that Rudy, now as mayor of a very liberal city, would have to pander to certain left-wing elements from time to time, but I certainly could not abide such behavior from a friend without so much as a phone call. I called Schwartz at home to complain about this. "What the hell does Rudy think he's doing?" I asked.

"Come on, Frank," Schwartz responded. "Banning books? You expect Rudy to support that?"

"What I expect," I replied, "is the courtesy of a phone call first from a friend, so that I can explain my position before he sticks the knife in my back. This is not about censoring books from adults. It's about tax money and children. Would Rudy let his kids read a book which described Columbus as a madman?"

"Uh, well......" he stammered.

"What about a book about homosexual techniques? Is Rudy a book burner if he would forbid the schools to show that to his kids?"

"Uh, well, Frank, what you have to understand is… well, Martin Luther King, come on..."

"I want to speak to Rudy about this," I insisted. "In fact, I want to ask him these very questions on the radio. If Rudy can fit bashing me into his busy schedule, then let's see him give me and *my* supporters equal time. Or are you afraid when I put him on the spot, he'll have to give in?"

Giuliani, like the rest of the politicians, would never permit himself to be debated by me in a fair forum and, of course, never did get back to me.

In addition to the usual diatribes about racism and hate, one of the main criticisms of my actions was that I was guilty of promoting censorship. Although I realized that it was useless to try and speak reasonably to a bunch of hysterical liberals who probably wouldn't even swerve their cars to avoid hitting me, I did attempt to explain my position, which, due to time and editing, I was able to do on radio and television talk shows, as opposed to newspapers and TV news.

The issue of censorship was, of course, preposterous. My plan to remove objectionable materials from the schools cannot be discussed without examining two crucial aspects of the plan. Although it was easy for the jackals to lump all banning of books under the category of censorship, my plan was yet another example of an issue which my hysterical critics could not deal with on a rational level. The first aspect of my proposal to remove anti-American, revisionist multicultural materials from the schools was very elementary: we are dealing with children. In the case of District 24, these children were aged 5 to 13. In no civilized society do children possess the same rights as adults. In no society do children make all of their own decisions and do whatever they want. Equating my ideas with removing books which adults wish to read from, say, the New York Public Library, was political nonsense. Children don't decide for children; adults decide for children, especially very young children. Even today, if a person under the age of 17 wishes to see an R-rated movie, an adult must accompany that minor. No one cries censorship over this. When I was 10 years old, my father would not let me read the novel "The Godfather," because of the violence and nudity. Needless to say, I had to do what my father said. There are so many examples of this, that the fact that the accusation of "book-burning" even held the slightest bit of currency only proved the irrational ideological zealotry of my opponents.

One of the most basic jobs of a parent is to prohibit; to forbid; to disallow; to censor; to *ban*. If any of my critics had ever forbidden their child from reading a book on how to make explosives, or on the wonders of bestiality, then, *by their own definition*, they were guilty of censorship. Ironically, my position was very pro-parent in the sense that I would support the right of any parent, provided they were not guilty of child abuse or of a crime, to do whatever they want with their own children. If individual parents were crazy enough to want their children to read such books, that was fine with me. But, as an elected member of a public school board, my position was: do it on your own time, with your own money. I did not want anti-American materials in the schools over which I had authority.

The second part of my plan was the aspect of taxpayer money. It is bad enough that multicultural trash is being given to children.

What makes it all the more reprehensible is that it is paid for by the general public. I frequently used the example of Senator Jesse Helms' criticism of the National Endowment for the Arts for using taxpayers' dollars to fund pornography. He too was accused of censorship, but was merely pointing out that these "artists" should be forced to use their own money if they wanted to show men with bullwhips in their rectums.

None of this made any difference to the racial hustlers and America-haters. As I pointed out in the statement I was to make, "censorship", of course, was relative. Some books, it seems, are more equal than others, and are more worthy of protection from censors like me.

That first night, the media and political storm was still only beginning. City politicians were all over the airwaves demanding my resignation. They were all galvanizing for the huge school board meeting in Corona in two nights. These calls for my resignation were something I always viewed as extremely laughable. (I did, in fact, laugh a great deal when they were stated publicly at the coming meeting.) More than anything else, they demonstrated the enormous gulf between "official" opinion and the views of the public at large, which judging by the supportive mail I was to receive and the tallies on election day, was overwhelmingly on my side. My critics were, in a sense, stymied by a very annoying technical point: I was elected. And unlike an appointed official who would have been fired for having expressed the views I did, my critics could do nothing about my presence on the board but yell and scream. The fact that I was elected not only prevented my removal, but it allowed me to point to genuine public support for my positions. But, according to my enemies, one voice of dissent was one too many. They simply had to destroy me and were planning on doing just that.

The morning after – which was now one day before the school board meeting – additional stories came out in the press. Two of the city's newspapers ran searing editorials. I did a morning radio talk show and another television news program, and then came the first prolonged television debate at noon. The show, "Street Talk," was aired live and was very popular. It was hosted by former New York

City mayor Ed Koch and a liberal reporter named Felipe Luciano. There was no audience, just four people sitting around a table for half an hour. My opponent was Perry Buckley. Now, the format of this daily program was a "left vs. right" debate, with Luciano and one guest forming the liberal side, and Koch and the other participant taking the conservative point of view. This time, however, the show would be a little different. On this occasion, Koch would be joining the liberals (where he always belonged in the first place) and it would be three against one.

The two hosts were somewhat receptive to my point that the middle class white communities were seething with anger over what they felt was the special treatment that minority groups are always getting. Cowardly politicians, I pointed out, are giving in to militant demands by every radical ethnic lobby, whether it be for special curriculum, government forms and elections ballots in different languages, and racial quotas in hiring. I explained that I represented these people and they had a right to a voice on the school board. This, I explained, was exactly how I got elected in the first place. "Well," Koch asked, "then why didn't the press pick up on you as the next David Duke?"

While Buckley, as a media neophyte, was rather restrained, he did support racial quotas in hiring. But what set the Gang of Three off more than anything else was my statement, from the original Newsday article, that "We are a white, Christian, British, Protestant nation." Koch, that great detective, was quick to point out that I was of Italian descent and Catholic. Again, this statement, which provided so much ammunition for the racial hustlers, is easily defensible as a current truth and can easily be documented as a historical reality of the United States. The United States was founded by British colonists. The *political* nation was always British in culture and mores. The beauty part about our British culture was that people from different backgrounds have been able to assimilate into the United States rather easily. At least this was true of the immigrants from Europe. Therefore, my statement was more of a cultural statement than necessarily a demographic one.

In Russell Kirk's book, "America's British Culture," he writes,

"So dominant has British culture been in America, north of the Rio Grande, from the seventeenth century to the present, that if somehow the British elements could be eliminated from all the cultural patterns of the United States – why, Americans would be left with no coherent culture in public or in private life... the transplanted culture of Britain in America has been humankind's more successful achievements... America's successes, substantially, have been made possible by the vigor of the British culture that most Americans now take for granted. Who, then, are the people desiring to pull down this dominant culture and set up in its place some amorphous 'multiculture'?"

Kirk goes on, "...whatever the racial or ethnic origins of Americans, the principal feature of the culture within which they have their being are British in origin." Kirk describes the four major "fashions" or folkways which have shaped American culture as 1. "the English language"; 2. "the rule of law, American common law and positive law being derived chiefly from English law"; 3. "representative government"; and 4. "a body of mores, moral habits and beliefs and conventions and customs, joined to certain intellectual disciplines."

This is exactly what the multicultural fanatics detest about America and what they wish to dismantle. Responding to my infamous statement, the New York Daily News, in an editorial published that morning entitled, "Alienation", sarcastically wrote, "A question for Mr. Borzellieri: Could you please point to the Borzellieris on the Mayflower passenger manifest?" (In a subsequent editorial they would refer to me as "the devil.")

In New York Newsday's editorial entitled, "Mr. Whitebread", they wrote, "If you ever want to see diversity in action, forget about the United Nations. Pay a visit to District 24 in Queens... This fast-growing area is maybe 50 percent Hispanic, 20 percent Asian and 5 percent black... And in all, district residents speak more than 100 languages. But the strangest language you'll hear there is the one that school board member Frank Borzellieri speaks. Borzellieri has a list of books he wants to ban from school libraries because, he believes, they prevent children from being proud Americans. 'We are a white, Christian, British, Protestant nation,' he rather defiantly declares. You have to wonder: Who does this guy think he is representing? The people of Queens or the people of Iowa?" Astonishingly, before "Street Talk" ended, Luciano spouted some Afrocentric nonsense in response, claiming democracy originated in Africa. Even Koch repudiated this garbage. Buckley was silent.

In the elevator after the show, I reminded Koch that as mayor, he once caused a big stir by refusing to give city employees a paid day off for the Martin Luther King holiday. That was a courageous act. Why now, was he defending King to the hilt? He responded that at that time, King's birthday was not yet a national holiday. Also, he said, workers could have taken the day, but would not have gotten paid. Fair enough, but my larger point was that it was the same extremists who went after him who were now blasting me. The details may have been different, but the vicious emotion of the critics was for the same reason: expressing any sort of opposition to King.

Friends and Enemies

By now there were many calls of support for me coming into the district office, in complete contrast to a politically safe but ridiculous statement by District 24's administration that "These books are educationally appropriate and we firmly believe they have a place in our schools' libraries." My public support was also in contrast to Cummins' absurd statement that, "There are no books in our district that distort history."

The next morning, as a blood-thirsty crowd awaited me at PS 19 for that evening's raucous school board meeting, I spoke on the phone with both Roy Innis and Herb London, joking about what was in store for me. Throughout the whirlwind of this very public controversy, with the exception of Roy and Herb, and radio hosts Bob Grant and Jay Diamond, I did not have the public support of one public or elected official – including so-called conservative Republicans in New York government. Although I was told of some who secretly agreed with me, they hid like chickens, more concerned with staying in the good graces of the liberal power elite than standing up for the true beliefs of their constituencies.

As the school board meeting was approaching, I did make calls to two conservative journals of opinion in order to apprise them of this controversy. Since National Review is based in New York there was no doubt they were fully aware of what was going on. Editor Rich Lowry told me the magazine was already in the process of supporting me. Geoffrey Morris, he said, had already written an editorial for National Review's "The Week" section. The editorial that eventually ran praised my idea to deport illegal aliens rather than spend tax money to cater to them. (Three weeks later, I was invited as a guest to speak at National Review's editorial lunch.)

Human Events, my favorite newspaper, to which I first subscribed in 1987, is a weekly based in Washington, D.C., so I wasn't as sure if they had heard about the news. When I spoke to editor John Gizzi, he asked that I fax him several news clippings of the past three days. He was very supportive as I was telling him the story, and then he asked the question I heard from many conservatives, "Where is Mary Cummins in all this?" (Human Events had written favorably of Cummins during the "rainbow" fight.)

I have always been amazed at conservatives who automatically assumed that Cummins was some kind of pillar of the conservative cause. Here was this old lady whom no one had ever heard of, and whom no one really knew much about. Like Cummins, the Wisconsin legislator Polly Williams, who was on the vanguard of the school choice movement, also became admired by conservatives. But everyone knew, outside of that one issue, that Williams was a very liberal person. She had, in fact, managed Jesse Jackson's 1988 presidential campaign in her state.

So as person after person expressed stunned amazement that Cummins was not supporting me in this and actually opposed me with a ridiculous pro-multicultural statement (she would make another one this night), I was becoming well-versed in rattling off the outrageously liberal things that Cummins had said. Gizzi listened to all of this intently and expressed great sympathy for my actions. We talked about the huge interview spread Human Events had done with Cummins. Gizzi was clearly dismayed at what I was going through and I sensed a certain betrayal that he felt about Cummins, especially after Human Events had supported her so openly. Maybe he felt more duped than betrayed. He wished me luck. Considering the events of the week, it meant a lot to have the support of National Review and Human Events.

Cummins would come to regret her vile opposition to me, since I was telling the truth about her to the only people who admired her, the conservatives. Although she would come to be thought of as a traitor by many conservatives, I didn't agree, for the simple reason that she was never one of us in the first place.

When media people, at my urging, did push Cummins on her hypocrisy – banning books like "Heather Has Two Mommies" while condemning "censorship" by me – she responded lamely, "That was different. We banned the whole curriculum." Oh, so banning books as part of a whole objectionable curriculum is different from just banning objectionable books. Poor Mary. The old lady was trying to dig herself out of a whole with conservatives that she could never quite get out of.

In the midst of the storm, I did manage to call Ramon Cortines, the chancellor of the New York City public school system. "I suppose by now," I said, "you know why I'm calling." I explained my position to him and he listened thoughtfully. Although he would not buy into my arguments entirely, he did say he respected my philosophy. "I understand that you have a constituency and are entitled to your point of view," he said. Although in other controversies, Cortines would come out more publicly and forcefully against me, he didn't, at least this time, resort to the insane rhetoric and accusations of my liberal enemies. Despite our profound differences, I respected him.

As I was gearing up for this big night, I was informed that over 40 speakers had called in to request speaking time at the meeting. The average number of speakers is usually about three to five. Every local politician would also be there (except for the cowardly Republicans.) Other than a handful of my own friends scattered throughout the auditorium, I would have no support there. The police had already been called in for extra security.

My Battle Against Multiculturalism

Two hours before the meeting, I was writing the statement that I would make that night. I called Garkowski and told him that due to the circumstances I did not want to take my own car to the meeting. I would park at his rectory and go with him.

Preparing for the long night, I took some papers with me, a copy of National Review, and Thomas Sowell's book, "Inside American Education." But I understood that the most important thing I would bring with me was my demeanor, my attitude. I knew that I was right on the issues. I also knew that no matter what this vicious, hateful crowd had in store for me, the sentiments of the silent majority – the true public at large – were all that mattered to me. Everything I would say, with the television cameras and radio and print media there, would be aimed at that true public. Bearing that in mind, I still knew the crowd would try to make this a lynching – an expectation that turned out to be well-founded. Although I would improvise some of my actions and comments on that stage, I knew that the best way to stick it to this hysterical lynch mob was to show them that they couldn't rattle me.

I would add that that did not require much effort or mental strategy on my part because it all came quite naturally to me. First of all, on the merits of the arguments and individual points on the issue, the debate would be no contest. I would have strong intellectual points; they would have crazed screaming and name-calling. But it had to be more than that. I had to be seen – outnumbered 400 to one – to be laughing *at them*. Although the meeting would turn out as vicious as I expected, I always knew that in spite of whatever vile forms of attack they had in store for me, in the end I would be the one left standing.

Liberal Freak Show

As Garkowski and I were driving to the meeting, it was a dank, chilly night in May, with drizzle coming down. Hollywood could not have prepared a better setting. Out of 24 schools in the district, this meeting just happened to be scheduled at PS 19 in Corona. It was the largest school in the district, thereby able to accommodate the most people, and the school from which I removed the books. It was also located in the district's multicultural heartland. As we were driving in the rain, underneath the elevated Number 7 train on Roosevelt Avenue, I could not believe what I was seeing. As we were still blocks from the school, there were giant television satellites lining all the streets. Police were stationed on every block for at least a quarter of a mile radius from the school. It was as if the president of the United States was arriving at the United Nations. When we finally parked the car about three blocks away, I got out and said to the cop stationed there, "I can't believe all of this is for me." He squinted at me in the rain, and then realized who I was. "You're the one who said those things about the books and Martin Luther King." He smiled and extended his hand. "Good luck," he said. I glanced at Garkowski to see his reaction; he remained totally expressionless.

As Garkowski and I were making our way to the school, several police officers surrounded me when school security told them who I was. As I entered, I saw the huge noisy crowd awaiting my arrival. I had to make my way through the center of the auditorium and climb the steps to the stage where the board was to sit. As I got to the stage, all the lights, cameras and reporters surrounded me. I told them I would be making a statement after the meeting started. Although the crowd was already jeering me, they really had no idea what I would do. I suspect they thought I would crack, back down, or perhaps backtrack on my position somewhat. From the stage, I waved vigorously to a few people I knew in the audience. Board president Mary Crowley pulled me aside. "I have to remove you as chairman of the curriculum committee," she said.

By now I was not surprised at any act of cowardice. Although Crowley's unseemly act was in complete circumvention of the will of the voters, it would turn out to be the least of her sins. As president of the board, she also chaired the meeting. The by-laws were very clear in stating that speakers at meetings may not use derogatory words about any person, and the person's name may not be mentioned. (Whether these rules were correct or practical, the fact remained that they *were* the rules, and were always enforced by Crowley and past presidents. Even the liberal press would point out the double standard in the coming days.) In addition, scheduled speakers were to be limited to five minutes, with unscheduled speakers limited to three minutes. But with Crowley chairing the meeting, and Sansivieri controlling the timer, the whole concept of rules and order became a farce. For four hours, speakers said the most vile things about me, and most of the time the timer was not even set. All the speakers against me, especially the politicians, were permitted to far surpass five minutes, with the whole fiasco becoming a very incendiary and dangerous affair.

In a full-page advertisement that would be taken out days later in the Times Newsweekly by some of my local supporters entitled, "The Liberal Lynching of Frank Borzellieri," the situation was described as "...one of the most disgusting spectacles in Queens history... when Community School Board Member Frank Borzellieri was torn apart by a liberal lynch mob in an auditorium full of radical left-wing interest groups and cowardly grandstanding liberal politicians."

Not only did Crowley allow this circus against all sense of decency and fairness, but she did it on the heels, two weeks earlier, of appointing me to chair an ad hoc committee on Family Living/Sex Education (where I could have an impact, along with chairing the curriculum committee, on the issues I was most associated with. Now she had removed me from all committees.) At that time, she told the Queens Tribune I was "in tune with the times. He grew up with many of the young parents in the schools."

It did not take long for the crowd of liberal freaks and misfits to begin their degenerate festivities. After the opening gavel was hit, and the Pledge of Allegiance was winding down, the foot-stomping crowd kept chanting the final two words of the Pledge. "For all! For all! For all!" they screamed. I couldn't help but crack a smile, which, needless to say, annoyed the crowd very much. In fact, my demeanor the entire evening would drive them crazy. Although I could not remember from what movie I heard the expression, I kept thinking, "What you choose to call hell, I call home."

The crowd was filled with such a peculiar assortment of left-wing misfits, that the audience could only be described as a Liberal

Freak Show. It included supporters of black supremacist Leonard Jeffries, who were decked out in full African garb with large photos of Jeffries on campaign-style buttons they were wearing. Also present were officials of the NAACP, the radical black organization which supports racial quotas and forced school busing. At that time, Ben Chavis was still head of the group, and had just aligned himself with Louis Farrakhan, who said all whites were "devils."

In addition, Norman Lear's People for the American Way was there, as well as Norman Siegel of the New York Civil Liberties Union, which has functioned as a virtual criminals' lobby, while supporting homosexual marriages. Also in attendance was the Queens Lesbian and Gay Pride Committee, a radical homosexual group founded by Daniel Dromm, a District 24 teacher who "outed" himself in front of his fourth grade class, supported the "rainbow" curriculum, and was recommended for disciplinary action for conduct unbecoming a teacher. There were many other left-wing oddball multicultural groups present, as was Ellen Levine, author of "I Hate English." Most conspicuous among liberal politicians was New York City's second highest-ranking elected official, Comptroller Alan Hevesi. Now Hevesi, a left-wing radical of the highest order, had been Grand Marshal of the Queens Lesbian and Gay Pride parade (where he wore a sash and marched with "drag queens" and transvestites.) As a state assemblyman, he voted against beginning sessions of the assembly with the Pledge of Allegiance. He also supported homosexual marriage and all sorts of extreme liberal causes.

(Years later, Hevesi would become Comptroller of New York State and would be arrested and forced out of office as part of a plea bargain to avoid indictment. Hevesi pleaded guilty to defrauding the government, a Class E felony, and paid a fine for bilking the state by using state employees as drivers and personal assistants for his wife. He also had to submit a DNA sample for the state's criminal databank and was forced to repay the state more than $200,000 for use of the employees.)

After a few minutes dispensing with procedural business, it was time for the main event. I told Crowley I had a statement to read, and as I began there were already obscenities and threats coming from the audience. Any thoughts by the crowd that I would capitulate were abandoned immediately upon the commencement of my statement. I was shouted down and continuously interrupted by vile remarks, including one by the head of an Irish lesbian group, who shouted, "You white supremacist!"

My entire statement was as follows: "Allow me to set the record straight – now. First, regarding the reporting of my statements and the statements themselves. My statements were reported accurately as far as what I actually said. However, some news accounts were incomplete. I had parents tell me they were interviewed and supported me, but never saw a word of it in print. This gives the false impression that I have no support. I would like to thank the various radio and television programs which respected my right of free speech and allowed me the opportunity to explain my statements fully, without distortions.

"Regarding my statement on the historical culture of America, my full statement is that America was a white Christian nation in its founding. The men who wrote the Constitution and rebelled against the British were responsible for the background, culture and mores of America at that time. The Judeo-Christian ethic has guided our nation for over 200 years. America remains guided by these principles. For decades, immigrants have come to America and assimilated into our culture. Everything from having Sunday as a day of rest to the presumption of innocence in the courts – uniquely Western concepts – emanate from the Eurocentric culture on which America was founded.

"In addition, I have spoken to the chancellor, a thoughtful man, and I explained to him that my position has nothing to do with the kind of 'censorship' that many have tried to portray it as. On this issue of censorship, I will state my position quoting my own words in a Newsday article back on March 10th. I said, 'I'm for printing and reading, buying and selling whatever you want.'

"What I am against and what I do oppose is spending taxpayer dollars on material with anti-American lies and teaching it to the children. We would not allow 'Heather Has Two Mommies' for obvious reasons. We should not allow a book that says Christopher Columbus was a terrorist and a madman.

"My position is similar to the one of Senator Jesse Helms regarding obscene art sponsored by the National Endowment for the Arts, where taxpayer dollars financed a work of 'art' showing a crucifix in a vat of urine entitled 'Piss Christ' and various photos of homosexuals using whips in an obscene manner. Senator Helms said if you want to create these things or go to a museum and look at these things, be my guest. But don't expect the taxpayers to pay for it. My position is the same regarding revisionist history.

"I explained my position not only to Chancellor Cortines but to Ralph Reed of the Christian Coalition. Others who really care about the details of my position should have called me before reacting in such a knee-jerk manner. But the fact is they really don't care. I had previously received a statement of support from Dr. Hebert London, the educational scholar, regarding my views on multiculturalism. Herbert London told me that in his seven year old daughter's school, she is taught the Puerto Rican national anthem, but not the Star Spangled Banner. And Herb had to buy the American flag for the school because they refused to get one.

"During the 1988 presidential primaries, Jesse Jackson led a chorus of multiculturalists in a chant of 'Hey hey, ho ho, Western culture's gotta go.' Does this concern you? It should.

"In New York State, Leonard Jeffries was one of the people commissioned by Education Commissioner Thomas Sobol to oversee the multicultural curriculum being written. Jeffries, of course, is the man who said blacks were superior to whites because of the melanin in their skin. He said the blacks were the 'sun' people and the whites were the 'ice' people. This is the man who is influencing the multicultural curriculum? Does this concern you? It should."
[Upon hearing these remarks, the supporters of Leonard Jeffries, seated in the front, began chanting some loud black supremacist rantings. They were yelling, "That's right!" and "Jeffries is right!" and "Black power!" I stopped in the middle of my statement, pointed to those radicals, and admonished the crowd, "These are the people you area aligning yourselves with?" I'll never forget all those white

liberals applauding the Jeffries people. The most incredible image was Alan Hevesi standing to the side smiling and applauding these freaks. Naturally, none of the officials there disavowed the Jeffries people.]

I continued my statement amidst constant heckling and insults. "My views on multiculturalism are identical to those of National Review magazine, which dedicated an entire issue to the subject. In it, John O'Sullivan writes, 'Multiculturalism regards assimilation as a form of oppression.' Linda Chavez writes, '…in the past, government – especially public schools – saw it as a duty to try to bring newcomers into the fold by teaching them English, by introducing them to the great American heroes as their own, by instilling respect for American institutions. Lately, we have nearly reversed course, treating each group, new and old, as if what is most important is to preserve its separate identity and space.'

"My views are also totally in agreement with those of Dr. Thomas Sowell, who states in his book, 'Inside American Education,' that 'The United States has been ethnically diverse for more than a century, yet successive massive waves of immigrants have arrived on these shores and become Americans without any such programs as have been proposed by the multiculturalists. Nor is there the slightest evidence… that the transition has gone better as a result of multiculturalism. The claim that groups will get along better when they are given multicultural education is a straightforward claim which might be straightforwardly tested against the facts – but it almost never is. The educational benefits of multiculturalism are likewise often proclaimed but seldom documented. There is no *a priori* reason to believe such claims, especially in the face of multiple evidences of declining educational quality during the period when multiculturalism has taken up more and more of the curriculum.'

"Rather than debate me on the merits of these arguments, liberals seek to attack my motives and character. Rather than refute my arguments, they resort to name-calling and accusations of bigotry. Two years ago, Pat Buchanan stated that one million Englishmen would be easier to assimilate than one million Zulus. He was also accused of bigotry. This is intended to stifle debate rather than examine Mr. Buchanan's cogent reasoning. Accusations of bigotry are still the last refuge of a scoundrel.

"Now, last November the NAACP tried to ban a book from the public schools in Fairfax, Virginia, because they deemed it offensive to blacks. So I guess what's good for the goose is not good for the gander. The NAACP can remove a book offensive to blacks, but I can't even question a book that degrades Western culture.

"I have my first amendment right of free speech. This is apparently of no matter to my detractors who would seek to silence me.

"But I have promises to keep. I made campaign promises to the people who elected me and I intend to keep those promises. While they may not agree with me, many of my critics have acknowledged that I do indeed have a following that elected me, in school board standards, by a landslide. What about my constituency? Don't they have a right to a voice on this board?

"Finally, we are tired. The Italian-Americans are tired. The German-Americans are tired. The Hungarians, the Irish, the Polish-Americans. We are all tired of racial quotas, of reverse discrimination, of not getting jobs even though we scored higher on a test. We came to America, assimilated and learned English. We are tired of those who refuse to do so. We are tired of every ethnic interest group demanding its own curriculum, and street signs and government forms in different languages. It was never done for any of us. Why should we do it now? We are tired of being made to feel guilty for the past grievances of so-called oppressed minorities. We never asked for special privileges. Stop asking for our dollars! Enough is enough.

"I would like to thank all those citizens and organizations who called the district office to offer support, approval and even financial assistance. It was greatly appreciated. On these matters I will never be silenced. Thanks you."

At one point during my statement, Sansivieri stood up and interrupted me. "Why don't you resign, Frank, for the good of the children?" she asked derisively, and to loud cheers.

"I have a better idea, Linda," I retorted. "Why don't you try and defeat me on election day?"

The noise became so loud toward the end of my statement, that I actually had to ask Crowley to silence the audience. When she refused to do so, I stood up with the microphone and said, "I'm going to finish this statement whether you like it or not!"

When I was finished, I thought the place was about to be set ablaze. Crowley told the audience, "Mr. Borzellieri's views do not reflect those of the school board's."

Cummins did not show up, claiming to be ill, but she did issue a brief statement which Crowley read. Cummins called my views "ridiculous," stating she was "appalled" at what I believe. She also said Martin Luther King was a "magnificent person." I would have loved nothing more than to show every decent person in America the videotape of all those liberal freaks cheering Mary Cummins on, from the bottom of their leftist hearts. How fitting.

The parade of speakers then began. In a four hour liberal hate-fest, some 40 speakers would carry on a charade worthy only of Ringling Brothers. The first speaker was Alan Hevesi, who said, "You took your bigotry and wrapped it in the American flag. That is a technique of the Ku Klux Klan." He also said my opinions were "ideologically incorrect," adding a new dimension to the strategy of the thought police. "You shouldn't take your ignorance and make that a standard in this district."

I responded, "I don't answer to liberal politicians."

Although Hevesi's arrest for defrauding the government came years after this meeting, the Hevesi angle of this affair did develop into an amusing side issue at the time – a development which demonstrated what a wimp and coward he really was. My actions were widely viewed as so important that Hevesi, the second highest-ranking official in New York City, took time out of his schedule to appear and denounce me in a room where I was outnumbered some 400 to one. But the next morning, I did the Bill Mazer radio show and I faxed a letter to both Mazer's producer and to Hevesi, challenging him to a fair one on one debate, on the air. The producer loved the idea and indeed offered to allow the debate live on air. He followed up with Hevesi's office, but Hevesi never responded to numerous faxes and phone calls.

Among the other local politicians who spoke was the radical black city councilwoman (and later Queens borough president) Helen Marshall. On the Martin Luther King issue, she said, "My God, young man, if you don't understand what greatness is and Martin Luther King's Nobel Peace Prize, then you shouldn't sit on this board... Where does such a young man get these ideas?" In response, I smiled and held up a copy of National Review and Thomas Sowell's "Inside American Education."

In fact, as speaker after speaker, including all the other board members, denounced me, the crowd was becoming very annoyed with my little antics. Holding up my materials, waving to people in the audience, and occasionally applauding speakers sarcastically, I was showing the crowd that they could not intimidate me, and conversely, that I was thriving on all the attention. At one point, I actually climbed down from the stage to shake hands with Melinda Katz, a state assemblywoman, who had just finished criticizing me. All this gave the impression that I was actually enjoying myself, in the same way one enjoys the slapstick of a Marx Brothers movie. They did not like that very much.

While all of this was going on, I remembered a small item I had read about ten years earlier, when William F. Buckley, Jr. was being sued by some oddball on the political fringe. To show his disdain for the entire ridiculousness of the situation and the total lack of importance that the encounter held for him, Bill Buckley sat in the courtroom reading a book while the proceedings were going on. I suddenly decided that my time would be better spent doing the same thing. I began reading Sowell's book, leaning back and holding the book high enough for all to see what I was doing. The crowd became enraged, with many screaming to Crowley that I not be permitted to read (as if they could stop me) and be forced to pay attention (as if they could force me.) I was subsequently told by friends in the audience that my perceived fearlessness and irreverence annoyed the crowd more than anything else. "Just look at him up there!" many were saying.

The Queens Tribune even ran a photo of me reading, with the caption, "Frank Borzellieri 'kept busy' while speakers criticized him." In their editorial the following week, they wrote that I "sat on the stage like a king on his throne. He ignored the comments of parents and others who addressed him, conducted news interviews in the middle of the hearing and averted the eyes of his critics by holding up a book to read instead."

The board members all had their say. Elizabeth Gambino, another left-wing extremist, said, "Anyone who says America is made up of an Anglo-Saxon point of view is a racist."

Jake LaSala, another white leftist who claims to love multiculturalism but shields himself and his family by living in a white neighborhood, said, "This sets us back one hundred years."

Louisa Chan said, "That ours is basically a Eurocentric culture is neither accurate nor realistic."

When Councilwoman Helen Marshall was speaking, she was badly butchering the pronunciation of my last name. She finally blurted out something resembling my name and hooted about how Italians should be made to change their names. The audience joined in the mocking delightedly. I took no particular offense since I certainly have a difficult name, but I remember thinking what would ever have happened if a white person had made fun of an African-sounding name? It would have been cause for another one of these meetings, I suppose.

After about twenty speakers, each of whom was permitted by Crowley to violate the rules of the board (not to mention the rules of civility), someone spoke in my defense. My friend Thomas Ballou, a former aide to a city councilman in a different district, went to the microphone with about four open books cradled in his arms and said, "Well, now that all the grandstanding is over, let me tell you all why Frank is right." The crowd was in shock. He quoted from Lawrence Auster's blistering critique of multiculturalism, "The Path to National Suicide," and admonished the crowd. "If it weren't for British influence on our laws, Frank Borzellieri would have already been dragged into the street and beaten," he said. Crowley soon cut him off, clearly not allowing him the full five minutes to which he was entitled. As he walked to the back of the auditorium to derisive comments and boos, the press converged around him. Two others would speak in my defense near the end of this fiasco, each being jeered and threatened by the crowd.

As the evening wore down, the intensity did not. One black man identified himself as a member of the NAACP. He remarked that I probably got elected because people didn't know my views. "For your information," I responded, "I'm the only board member who gave the voters a true representation of my views. By the way, is the NAACP still supporting racial quotas and forced school busing?"

"Uh, that's irrelevant right now," he answered uncomfortably.

When the final speaker finished at around one o'clock in the morning, and Crowley banged the gavel to adjourn the meeting, I grabbed the mike one last time, stood up and said, "Nice try!" I was once again surrounded by reporters who wanted my take on the evening. My final comments were that we had just witnessed a Liberal Freak Show, and despite the efforts of everyone in the room, I vowed to win re-election to the board by an even bigger margin than the first time. As I was speaking, there were still taunts coming from the dispersing crowd. Although frustrated by their inability to rattle me, I assumed at that point that the consensus was that I was finished – both politically and as someone who would continue to speak out on these issues. These were assumptions, to the liberal fanatics' utter dismay, that would shortly prove to be very wrong. Not only would I never be silenced, but the public support would come rolling in after the evening's meeting made the television news, not to mention the radio and newspapers.

Even locally, the ad entitled, "The Liberal of Lynching of Frank Borzellieri," aroused the angry passions of decent people. In addition to naming all the politicians who were present, and castigating the other board members and left-wing organizations, the ad stated, "At the Board meeting, Frank was savaged in the most cruel, ignorant and senseless manner by hysterical left-wing radicals who shouted, screamed vulgar accusations at him and would not allow him to speak. These liberal freaks demanded Frank's resignation for having the nerve to dare to speak the truth out loud, and called him every vile name in a dangerous circus atmosphere. Frank's supporters were shouted down and threatened and Frank needed a police escort out of Corona back to his home in Ridgewood."

When I was leaving, six plainclothes policemen surrounded me and walked me back to the car. They were laughing and slapping me on the back. "You have balls," one of them said. "How the hell could you stand all that?" I was subsequently told by a friend that all the cops, speaking amongst themselves, were cheering me on. They followed Garkowski and me back to the rectory, where they then followed me all the way home. When I got out of my car at home, the cops were still laughing and wishing me luck, and the one in the front passenger seat said, "Man, you had them completely overmatched."

There are so many stark images and memories that I will forever have etched in my mind from that night, but perhaps what I will remember most vividly are the sadistic expressions of hate on the faces of board members and in the crowd. It was not enough to berate me. They had to permanently silence and destroy me. But they outsmarted themselves. Because, as the saying goes, what doesn't kill me makes me stronger.

Support comes rolling in

The controversy still would not die. New York Newsday wrote, "But even excoriated, Borzellieri did not back down…" Letters were still pouring into the district office overwhelmingly in my favor, to the chagrin of the rest of the board. Calls in support also would not stop. I was receiving unsolicited donations and even a postcard from a doctor with only one word printed on the back – in red, white, and blue – it said, "BRAVO!"

While the entire week was transpiring, there was still one radio show that I had not yet done, the top-rated Bob Grant program in the afternoon. All week, people were calling me to tell me what Bob and his callers were saying. Now Bob Grant was the most blunt, honest radio host in New York. More importantly, he was honest on the issues on which people are the most dishonest, race and culture. He had, many times, come under fire for criticizing Martin Luther King. "Bob Grant just nominated you for chancellor," one friend told me. "Bob Grant called you a hero," said another. It was now Friday, the day after the meeting, and although I had yet to speak to him, it was very clear that while I was spending the week being lynched by fanatical liberals, it was Bob Grant, every day, who was defending me, praising me and making sure my message was getting out. And it was getting out to millions of people. His callers were also supporting me to the hilt. Toward more than anyone else, on a public but also a personal level, my gratitude to Bob Grant was very deep and heartfelt. No one can know what it's really like to be under such vicious attack, compounded by the feeling of abandonment by so many public people who should have been supporting me, but instead ran for the tall grass. But Bob Grant was always there like the rock of truth.

As I was finally doing the show, Bob encouraged me to "keep doing what you're doing." I ripped into all those white liberal politicians from the previous night's meeting who live in safe lily-white neighborhoods, challenging them all to a fair debate. Bob said, "You're not only smart, you have courage." I vowed to continue my fight while exposing those cowardly school board members for the extreme liberals that they are, and their obscene penchant for squandering taxpayer dollars on multicultural trash. Finally, Bob offered me access to his show any time I needed the airwaves. Buoyed by the support of Bob and his listeners, I ended the interview with a message. "For all those who think their attacks on me will hinder or inhibit me, or stop me in any way from continuing my fight, I have a little message for you: I'm only *beginning*."

(Little did Bob know, six months later he would be made to endure an almost identical crucible, with New York Magazine running a front-page story titled, "Bob Grant: Why He Hates Blacks." As with me, those public figures who should have been supporting him the most, would run for cover.)

As the days went by, mail continued to pour in. There were basically two kinds of mail. Those in favor of my actions, from average citizens, and those opposed to me, from politicians and pointy-headed multicultural education gurus. What made this funny was that letter writers didn't realize that all mail sent to the board office was copied to all other members, so everyone saw everyone else's mail. Other board members were dying seeing all this mail supporting me.

Mark Green, the far left public advocate of New York City, wrote to the board, "I am sure you...agree that Mr. Borzellieri's racist remarks have no place in New York City public schools or anywhere else."

Whew! Glad he straightened me out about that. Green also wrote, "Instead of banning these books, Mr. Borzellieri ought to check them out of the school library, take them home and read them – carefully. He needs to embrace the cultural themes espoused in these books and work on dispelling his own ignorance." Now Mark Green had obviously been on another planet while the week's events were going on. It was precisely because I *had* "checked" out the books and read them "carefully" that I wanted to eliminate them.

The National Coalition Against Censorship wrote, "We must protect, preserve, and promote our libraries (and especially our school libraries) as centers for the free exchange of ideas... Fair and formal procedures for book selection and review should be scrupulously followed." Now, this is absolute nonsense. There is no "free exchange" of ideas in the public schools, nor are there "fair and formal" procedures for selecting books because it is liberals who control the entire process. They do not allow conservative or even moderate books to enter the schools. To the left-wing multicultural bureaucrats who censor pro-American books and ideas, the only kind of "free exchange" they want, is a free exchange of liberal books. As I will show in another chapter, some books are indeed more equal than others.

I did receive a letter from someone from Brooklyn, which demonstrated far better than I ever could the need to focus on the three r's and the basics of learning rather than multicultural babble. These excerpts are printed exactly as they were written: "'Young Martin's Promise' is very much American , this man's life was all

American he was born sergragation knew that was wrong he fought for the right to make it right for all man to be equal in his fight he was killed... What you are promoting is pure stupitdy... You are racist ignorent man who needs to be impeached, belive me I will do my part a see that you will no linger have that position very long. You need to learn that white is not always right."

Someone with roughly the same intelligence as this letter writer was a local liberal Democrat state assemblyman named Joseph Crowley (who later became a U.S. congressman), another white liberal who loves multiculturalism except when it comes to the neighborhood he chooses to live in. He also happened to be the nephew of board president Mary Crowley. Although I have my doubts as to whether Joseph Crowley (who was called a "dim bulb" by the liberal newspaper Newsday) authored the letter himself, it is within the realm of possibility that he did pick up a crayon and scribble something together. In a letter addressed to his aunt, but distributed to all board members, he wrote, "When the founding fathers of our country developed our system of government, they realized that for our country to thrive and flourish, its citizens must have the rights to discuss and express a full range of ideas without fear of repercussion."

I could not believe what I was reading. After all, it was Joe Crowley's aunt who was more responsible for suppressing my "rights" to discuss my ideas than anyone else. Talk about "fear of repercussion"! Was he kidding? Perhaps his aunt should put him through what I was made to endure simply because he wrote an imbecilic letter. Now Joe Crowley is more a man to be laughed at than taken seriously, but the double standard he espouses is so blatant, that even liberal newspapers could not ignore what Mary Crowley had done.

In reporter Rose Kim's column in Newsday, she referred to a board meeting two months prior, in which Mary Crowley immediately banged the gavel, ruling a speaker out of order and having security guards remove the man when he spoke the name and criticized a different board member. Regarding my situation, Kim wrote, "For some unexplained reason, board president Mary Crowley waived a board by-law that forbids public speakers from naming board members or criticizing their competence." The column continued, "...it's a mystery why Borzellieri was not given the same courtesy. [The man who had been removed] said he was stunned to hear speaker after speaker freely cite Borzellieri's name. Crowley did not return repeated calls to New York Newsday."

It was, of course, no mystery at all. As a charter member of the intolerant liberal thought police, Mary Crowley was obeying the informal by-laws regarding conservative opposition: one voice of dissent is one too many.

Two local Queens newspapers had to first, of course, extrapolate on the evils of my crusade before getting to the issue. The Queens Ledger wrote in an editorial titled, "Two Standards at School Board," "Borzellieri's actions are... areas of concern to us all... seemed appalling and dangerous to most of us. What seems worse to many of his critics are his constant ultra-conservative controlling attitudes in education."

The editorial continued, "It is obvious that the team in control of the School Boards [sic] voting block doesn't feel Mr. Borzellieri deserves to be recognized as a board member any longer... speaker after speaker verbally assaulted Borzellieri... What happened to being out of order? Was it that Borzellieri is on the wrong side of the School Board's Political power?"

The Queens Chronicle opined, "...if Borzellieri was not allowed to express himself in an open forum in an atmosphere of safety and respect, this was wrong." Its columnist Ernest Naspretto added, "Kaleed Muhammed gets to impart his true racist rhetoric on college campuses. Yet, an elected school board member cannot express his views on a controversial topic..."

Other editorials were not so kind. The Queens Tribune wrote, "Frank Borzellieri's performance at last week's School Board meeting was repugnant and disgraceful... Fortunately for him, there is no provision under which Borzellieri, elected to the board in May, can be removed... For the remainder of the term, however, it will be difficult to believe that Borzellieri's best interests lie with children and not with himself." The Times Newsweekly said I "came across as a fool and a crackpot" and stated that "New York City thrives on 'multiculturalism.'"

For the record, as long as I was quick to point out the racial hypocrisy of white politicians and school board members, it is equally true of all Queens newspaper owners and publishers. All of them are white liberals who editorialize on the "strength" and crucial importance of racial integration and multiculturalism, and who constantly remind us that Queens is such a wonderfully diverse borough, yet these owners and publishers themselves all live in lily-white areas, safely apart from the non-whites they claim add such strength to a community. I assume this to be true of the publishers of the major dailies, but regarding the Queens newspapers I know it for a fact. Once again, "integration for thee, but not for me."

While "official" opinion continued to be against me full throttle (television station New York 1 named me the "Loser of the Week". At year's end, the Village Voice would tap me as one of the ten "Losers of the Year"), the letters from average people were heartening. Most were addressed to me, but some to the board as a whole or to Mary Crowley.

"I, a working taxpayer who has lived in the community for over 40 years want Frank Borzellieri re-instated to the jobs he was legally elected to [meaning the curriculum committee which Crowley removed me from.] What has happened to him is a disgrace. What is happening to the American people is a disgrace. What has happened to C.S.B. #24 is a disgrace. I want it stopped!" said one letter.

Another said, "When I first read about your stand in regards to 'anti-American' books I said, 'It's about time.' I fully support your stance. There are a lot more of us than most people realize."

Yet another said, "...we wish to congratulate you on having the balls to stand up and voice your true American opinion on the subject of Americans learning how to speak English and read and write same *before* the bureaucrats begin spending taxpayers' money on books written in foreign languages. When [my husband's] parents came to this country from Europe some 60 years ago, they immediately learned how to speak the English language. We... stand wholeheartedly behind your efforts. We believe most Americans feel the same way as you and we do need a voice such as yours in order to be heard. Don't abandon your principles. You have a lot of moral support."

More local mail stated, "Mary Crowley [says she] believes in democracy and free speech, but yet viciously silences and illegally removes a bonafide elected official... Mr. Borzellieri was elected by his constituents with full knowledge of his proposed agenda... Miss Crowley, this is not Cuba or Haiti, this is the United States of America, and in this great country of ours we have freedom of speech!"

Another wrote to me, "You are 100 percent right and I support you all the way and all the people I know do too. They are destroying America are these liberals." Another wrote, "Today, reading the N.Y. Post, I saw them call you 'controversial.' Is it controversial today to speak about our commonality as Americans? Thank you for your work and your patriotism." Still another wrote, "From the bottom of my heart, I say a hearty, loud THANK YOU."

A letter to Crowley stated, "See to it that Frank is restored to his committees. He has the same right as you and everyone else. He speaks the truth and you know it. I am surprised at you. Do you like what [Leonard] Jeffries says. He is talking about you, too. Or are you too dumb to understand?"

Another supporter said, "There are many others who feel as I do. Keep up the good work and don't let yourself be silenced by the new wave of immigrants who clamor for freebies..." Another said, "Congratulations! Finally, there is a bright light in the community school board who realizes that multicultural curriculum is a consummate failure." Another local resident wrote, "I am both sad and angry to read about the shocking treatment towards Frank Borzellieri... he stands for the values I care about."

Another letter sent to the board office was also printed in the Times Newsweekly. Written by Glendale resident Catherine Knett, it stated, "It took me some time to recuperate from the political slaughter of Frank Borzellieri by a vicious mob of degenerates and cowardly politicians who were afraid to come to his defense at P.S.

19 in Corona last month. Now that I have sufficiently caught my breath I'd like to shout 'Three Cheers for Frank Borzellieri,' and ask where the hell are all the decent people who should have come to his support?

"Children, being children, need guidance... Schools have the obligation to provide a curriculum that will produce intelligent, law-abiding and self-sufficient citizens who will carry this country proudly into the 21st century. Needless to say, included in this curriculum must be proper reading material. To infiltrate schools and their libraries with books that are potentially dangerous to young, impressionable minds of children is subversive behavior... we [must have] the proper censorship so necessary for the protection of our children in order to weed out the decadent and evil reading material which the left-wing, flag-burning liberals would love to see promoted in our schools under the disguise of 'free speech.'

"If we allow such books as 'I Hate English' to occupy the shelves... then we must also make available for children's reading pleasures books on suicide, devil worship, the beauty of homosexuality, how to overthrow a government, sex with explicit pictures, etc... Frank Borzellieri is trying to prevent such a catastrophe. He is trying to guide our children back on the right path. He is trying, through our children, to save our country. Parents should be grateful to Frank Borzellieri, and be willing to support him in his efforts... So, people of Queens, for your children's sake, take an active interest in their reading material and don't be afraid of defying leftist mob rule."

These letters received in the school board office and cited here, which are distributed to each member and which represent a sample of a larger total, undoubtedly shook the rest of the board up very much. They saw with their own eyes not only the fact that my support was so wide, but that it was so deep, so passionate. This was not exactly what they had in mind when they began their vicious attacks on me from the time I was first elected, and especially through this controversy.

The Fight Continues

I came to realize that there were also some middle of the road people who were unclear about the issue until I explained it to them. The words "censorship" and "racism" had arisen so often in this debate, that at times I spent more time than I wanted answering those words. Indeed, many people still simply had a mistaken impression of exactly what multiculturalism is. I came across this on the Geraldo Rivera show, when certain callers asked what was wrong with learning about other cultures. In situations like this, I have always had to elaborate on the inherent anti-Americanism of multicultural education before I made the point that American culture should be stressed for no other reason than, well, this is America.

In addition to pounding away at the evils of multiculturalism, I continued to blast the left-wing groups that tried to silence me. I wanted to put *them* on the defensive by revealing their sorry records and saying, "See, these are who my critics are. Do you stand with them?"

Geraldo, who conducted a very fair show, nearly passed out when I called the NAACP a "liberal freak organization." When the bogus issue of "censorship" was raised again, I referred to the real issue of parental authority, stating, "If I could choose what I wanted to read when I was ten years old, I'd have read nothing but baseball cards." A Florida state legislator, Tom Feeney, who was on the show via satellite, certainly stood with me and gave more to the side of common sense and morality than did any New York politician. He would become a big help to me when I tried to implement an American cultural superiority resolution, which I will explain in the next chapter.

Another television talk show, "A+ For Kids," hosted by Richard Bey, became a circus when once again I was portrayed as the devil incarnate. A mostly minority audience of high school students had a great time lambasting me. The most significant moment of the show came when everything I had based my arguments on manifested itself. Bey asked for a showing of hands for all those proud of their ethnic backgrounds. Every hand in the audience went up. He then asked how many were proud to be Americans. Perhaps one quarter of the hands went up. "This proves my point!" I said loudly. How this could be lost on anyone I cannot imagine. These teenagers, all of whom were born here or certainly raised here, had more loyalty and identification with the country of their ancestors than the country of their citizenship – where they were living and raised, the United States. It is simply a fact – an uncomfortable fact for many people, but a fact nonetheless – that non-whites on average simply have less of an affinity for, loyalty to, and identification with their "American-ness."

When a black student made a derogatory comment about my views, I responded saying that today's non-European immigrants do not feel the same impetus to assimilate into American society as the immigrants of old did. With the black student standing up next to him, Bey thought he had me. "Frank, he's not an immigrant! And I'll bet his people are here longer than yours!"

With the crowd cheering, I responded, "That makes it worse! His people are certainly here longer than mine. So he should be *more* proud to be an American." The young man did not realize that he was about to make my point for me when he responded, to Bey's dismay, "That's right. I'm not proud to be an American. I'm sick of Dolly Madison and apple pie."

This issue of immigrant groups identifying with their own background and culture rather than with their land of citizenship (or at least the land where they reside), the United States, is one of the main reasons to oppose multiculturalism and one of the worst effects of it. Fanatical multiculturalists irrationally state the opposite – that it is the obligation of America to abet the dilution of American culture by ignoring it or denying its very existence, while focusing on and catering to every third world culture instead.

After all I had been through in such a short time, I looked forward to meeting with the editorial board of National Review as their invited guest at an editorial lunch in Manhattan. I was now meeting with so many of the people I had come to admire over the years and whose articles and opinions I was very familiar with as a long-time subscriber. Editor John O'Sullivan, Richard Brookhiser, Larry Kudlow, Linda Bridges, Rich Lowry and others all gave me their support, which was very important to me on a moral level, especially since all the so-called conservative politicians were nowhere to be found when I needed them. The National Review crowd understood that on the local, grass-roots level I was the one carrying the educational ball on matters the magazine cared about. I gave them a complete rundown of my ordeal, other than what they had seen and heard in the news. In a discussion of the Martin Luther King issue, senior editor Brookhiser made the point that although King did have communist affiliations, he was actually referencing the Declaration of Independence when he made the "I Have a Dream" speech. I pointed out that the details of King's activities were practically rendered unimportant in regards to my specific controversy because of the way liberals had behaved, which I explained in detail. The issue, I said, was political correctness. If we as conservatives cannot say what we want or believe, and must adhere to the liberals' notion that King is above criticism, then we are defeated. Obviously, Brookhiser agreed. We cannot, I stressed, allow this to happen or all we have worked for would be for nothing.

More Dragons to Slay

As the whirlwind of publicity was leveling off, many liberal educators were still reeling from my having exposed what exactly was going on in the district. As if I did not have enough to already complain about, the board was set to approve yet another one of those multicultural curriculum guides. Now, they were on pins and needles regarding what I might do. Although I would, at least until the next election, continue to be outnumbered on the board, my strategy had worked. To the horror of the totalitarians on the board and in the establishment, I had succeeded in going over their heads and appealing directly to the public.

On multiculturalism, this new guide stated, "...sexism, racism and biased attitudes toward the physically challenged harms young children and inhibits their development." It also stated "multicultural education values cultural pluralism and rejects the view that schools should seek to melt away cultural differences or merely tolerate cultural diversity; rather, multicultural education accepts cultural diversity as a valuable resource that should be preserved and extended." It should "identify the impact of racism and other barriers to acceptance of differences."

If this claptrap is not an overt appeal to balkanization, what is? Revisionist history also got a plug when the guide stated a goal as "to develop a multicultural perspective (interpreting history and culture from a variety of perspectives.)" The multicultural classroom should do this by "providing and displaying records, books, posters, magazines, and tapes that are free of bias and that reflect many cultures, languages, and different ways of life." The contrived socialist black holiday "Kwanzaa" was given equal time with "Earth Day." (Christmas and the Fourth of July were not mentioned.) Even on a non-ideological topic like different architectural types of bridges, the guide stated bridges "develop connections between diverse groups (race, color, national origin, gender, age, sexual orientation, disabling conditions) and to promote the development of positive group relations."

I realized from this new guide, along with everything else, that the battle would continue to be arduous, painstaking and cruel. The opposition to me would continue to be fierce and brutal, but so would my own determination. Unfortunately, within the district, those who have the greatest power to make the difference – the principals, teachers, administrators and librarians who secretly agreed with me – would remain silent. Socrates said that men by nature are slaves. I also believe in a slight variation of this, namely, that people are by nature conformist cowards. Their fear of being called "racist" and the ostracism they would face rivals only the fear of death itself. The silence by the very people in the best position to support my complaints was in stark contrast to the total lack of inhibition or fear shown by my totalitarian enemies. Indeed, this silence is a major contribution to the dispossession of America by fanatical multiculturalists, who are leading the country down the road to educational and cultural ruin.

But this multicultural controversy and the publicity it received were responsible more than anything else for blowing the lid off the "Myth of District 24," the patently false but previously widely-held notion that the school board of District 24 was "conservative." It was the voters and district citizens, not the board members, who deserved that label. And they now knew that I was their only voice on the most famous school board in the country. The public was now becoming aware that the district was not only adhering to an extreme liberal philosophy and squandering its tax dollars, but was perverting the minds of American children.

Having turned the tables on this bunch of losers with the support of the public, I realized that I had them on the run. There were more multicultural dragons to slay. Certainly, the fierce opposition would never relent, but neither would I. If there was to be a cultural war in this district, then I would be the one defending the home team. It was time to make the district face an issue it dreaded, the issue of American cultural superiority.

American Cultural Superiority

Before the radical liberals had the chance to catch their breaths, and before they could erroneously swallow the misguided notion that they somehow had been successful in subduing or quieting me down, literally within days the next opportunity was before me.

In Lake County, Florida, a controversy was brewing over a school board resolution which passed, mandating that history teachers teach that American culture is superior to all other cultures.

The wording of the resolution was: "In compliance with state law, the District School Board shall provide inservice training, media and instructional materials that explain and teach about other cultures. [This opening sentence was intended to assure that the district's curriculum complied with Florida state law, which mandated multicultural education. But the law did not preclude also teaching about American culture. Hence, the remainder of the resolution.] This instruction shall also include and instill in our students an appreciation of our American heritage and culture such as: our republican form of government, capitalism, a free-enterprise system, patriotism, strong family values, freedom of religion and other basic values that are superior to other foreign or historic cultures."

The sponsor of the resolution, board Chairwoman Pat Hart, was coming under attack from the usual cast of leftist characters. A local news article in Lake County began, "It's been called racist by some and vague by others, but Pat Hart says the policy she wrote stresses that students should learn that America is superior to all other cultures is crystal clear and doesn't warrant the fuss."

Hart was quoted, "I think the policy speaks for itself. Why would anyone have a problem with teaching America is the best country in the world?"

Ah, if such self-evident reasoning were simply accepted by the radicals. But Hart's question would inevitably be answered in several ways, as she would find out, and as I would also find out when

I proposed the same policy in District 24.

Two reasons that immediately jump out as to why people would "have a problem" with teaching the obvious is first, many "Americans" and resident aliens hate America, and second, many people living within the borders of the United States, whether citizens or not, possess loyalties to countries other than the United States. Many in this latter group may be "Americans" in the legal sense, but emotionally and in terms of their deepest felt attachments, they are not true Americans. Whether some observers are nervous about stating this out loud is not my problem. Everyone knows it's true, and I would have no trouble expressing it again when the situation warranted it.

Hart continued, "When we came, we were assimilated to the nation of America. And America was founded on governmental principles. I think our students need to be aware of that. They need to have the utmost knowledge and appreciation and understanding of our founding documents, our founding fathers, the principles of America and why America is great. We need to know that… Thousands of people risk life and limb every day to come to America because they know this is the land of the free."

Another Lake County board member, Judy Pearson, said, America is "the best of the best… Our form of government is superior to other nations' because it has survived when others have fallen."

In Lake County, those who opposed the resolution, including, as Hart called them, the "radical teachers union," were of the same mindset of those who would oppose me in District 24.

Florida State Education Commissioner Doug Jamerson stated unbelievably that the resolution was at odds with state requirements! Was it really possible that Florida law prohibited teaching that America is the best? Jamerson said, "To say American culture is superior to all others calls into question the rich history and significant contributions of all other nations and cultures whose influences shaped this country."

Where to begin? Even taking Jamerson's words as true (which I don't), that other cultures have a "rich history" and those cultures' "influences shaped this country," then Hart's resolution could actually be taken as *praising* other cultures, but otherwise stating that America's was best.

But Jamerson was just engaging in double talk regarding a policy he simply didn't like.

There was more mumbo jumbo coming from Keith Mullins, a liberal Florida activist, who said, "People don't understand the purpose and the point of this. We are already teaching our children to love and honor our country, so why spend all this time and money talking about something we are already doing? We've become sort of a laughingstock."

To which Hart replied – perfectly, I would add, "If we are already teaching these things, then there should be no opposition to this, and no problem, should there?"

When the issue became national news, it was generally regarded by normal people the same way, as in, what's the big deal? Aren't these things obvious, self-evident, and already being taught? Uh, well, no, not in Lake County and certainly not in District 24.

Two national columnists who normally are at odds with each other, Abe Rosenthal of the New York Times and Pat Buchanan, both agreed that it should be taught that America is best.

Buchanan wrote, "Of course, Western culture, of which American culture is a part, is superior. When the European explorers arrived here, the Aztecs were still into human sacrifice, and the locals had not yet invented the alphabet or the wheel. To call all cultures 'equal' is Political Correctness at the expense of truth."

Indeed, this strange desire to show "sensitivity" to other cultures has manifested itself in some shocking ways. When a Chinese immigrant beat his wife to death with a hammer for being unfaithful, a New York judge sentenced him to probation only, citing "cultural differences" as an excuse for the man's atrocity. In San Francisco, statutory rape charges were dropped against an Iraqi native who had sex with an 11 year old (an accepted practice in Iraq) because the district attorney "did not want to put the man's culture on trial."

Since 1965, Africa has become a measurable source of

immigration, and we are brow-beaten into "respecting" African culture. So what are Africa's current norms and historic culture? Female genital mutilation remains a custom in much of the Dark Continent. Gross national product per person is less than $200 a year. Africans have never built a modern economy. While the total number of children, grandchildren and great-grandchildren that the average American woman will have is 14, the equivalent figure for the average African woman is 258!

Before European colonization, no African society had devised a written language or discovered the wheel. None had a calendar or built multi-story buildings. They could not domesticate animals and had never produced a mechanical device. Africans had no concept of the biological origins of disease and attributed personal misfortune to the work of evil spirits. Similarly, before the European conquest of the New World, many Indians practiced infant sacrifice and had not discovered the wheel.

Today, the Laotian custom of kidnapping child-brides is practiced in the United States. Voodoo and witchcraft are now practiced to such a large degree in American cities with populations from Mexico, Central America and the Caribbean that numerous stores have emerged that carry everything needed to cast a spell, remove a hex or heal a mental disorder.

The courthouse in Dade County, Florida is constantly littered with dead animals, offered as ritual sacrifice by the city's Caribbean population as part of the practice called Santeria. Dead chickens, goat heads and lizards with their mouths tied shut are swept up daily by maintenance workers dubbed the "Voodoo Squad." Local Americans tried to charge the practitioners of these barbaric acts with animal cruelty, but the courts, citing "cultural respect," ruled them protected forms of religion.

Practitioners of something called "Palo Mayombe" rob graves and medical warehouses for human organs, mutilate and drink the blood of tortured animals and especially prize human sex organs, which they believe give them special powers.

But of course, all cultures are equal.

When I announced that I would be putting an almost identical version of the resolution on the agenda for our next board meeting, the national story became even bigger. With the resolution having passed in Lake County and having been proposed in District 24, the anticipated controversy was already causing a storm. I appeared on the Geraldo Rivera show with five other guests, three on each side of the issue. Geraldo, who was very fair to me, did ask me if I "really believed this stuff" (my views on multiculturalism and that the NAACP was a "freak" organization. I responded with the one word "yes," unlike some cowards who speak the truth, then backtrack.)

As the six of us battled it out, I praised guest Tom Feeney of Florida, congratulating him on having a sensible school board down in Lake County and lamenting that I wished we had those types of board members in New York. (Interestingly, Feeney, who was a nationally unknown member of the Florida House of Representatives at the time, later rose to prominence when he became Florida's point man in the Gore-Bush battle over Florida's electoral votes in 2000. By then, Feeney had become Speaker of the House and was attempting to certify Florida's electoral votes for Bush through the state legislature. Today, he is a United States congressman.)

One of the themes that kept recurring in the discussion was that somehow the policy denigrated other cultures. Now, that is a matter of interpretation. Saying one thing is the best is not necessarily saying the other thing is bad. But the true interpretation was that the anti-Americans in all this simply despised America and preferred criticizing America in the curriculum and focusing on other cultures.

The next day, Feeney and I consulted on the phone, and he faxed me some background information to help me form my wording for the resolution. He also told me that members of the Lake County school board and other supporters who saw the show told him they "wish they had that guy from New York" they had seen on the Geraldo show "on our school board."

The key point about the resolution was that it spoke in broad generalities, espousing things that no serious person could dispute. For example, the resolution did not speak to any particular policy, like for example, saying tax cuts were better than taxes being raised, or the death penalty was better than life in prison. The resolution

American Cultural Superiority

affirmed that the very basic ideals of Western Civilization and American culture were superior – things all Americans could agree on. Of course, freedom is superior to communism; the right to worship freely is superior to religious oppression, etc. But the Left was having none of it.

This controversy would place District 24 board members in an incredibly awkward position. I had already gotten word that Cummins, who was already feeling heat from having opposed me on the multicultural issue a month earlier, would not show up at the meeting. I was also told that she was working behind the scenes to see how they could torpedo the resolution procedurally, without having to vote on it.

In the meantime, I did the Bob Grant radio show, where he asked me to read my resolution on the air. It read, in part, "Resolved, that this School Board shall implement a district-wide policy mandating that our students be instructed, through appropriate books, materials, lectures, and lessons, that our American heritage and culture – such as our republican form of government, capitalism, a free enterprise system, patriotism, strong family values, freedom of religion, and other basic values that are uniquely American and Western – are clearly superior to all other foreign or historic cultures.

"The major problem facing our curriculum is moral relativism – the notion that all cultures are equal and that there are no objective truths. A parent testified before a United States Senate committee that her child was confused as to the 'rightness or wrongness' of stealing because of a 'values clarification' course she had taken. Similarly, the teaching of cultures has taken on the evil aspect of moral relativism, where no objective truths are taught regarding the obvious and objective superiority of American culture. We reject the notion that all cultures should be taught in an atmosphere of moral equivalency. We reject moral relativism and state unequivocally that American culture is superior to other cultures; that capitalism is superior to socialism; that freedom of religion is superior to religious oppression; that Adam Smith is superior to Karl Marx; that George Washington is superior to Che Guevera; that the Bill of Rights is superior to all foreign and historical constitutions; that guidance by the Ten Commandments is superior to paganism; and that American history and the American way of life are clearly superior to all others.

"We believe the objectivity of this view is self-evident, as revealed in truthful history and as revealed in the fact that people from all corners of the globe have sought to come to America… The children of District 24 shall not be denied this truth."

When I finished reading it, Bob asked incredulously, "How in the world can anyone possibly oppose that resolution?"

I responded, "If I knew the answer to that, I'd be making a million dollars a year as a psychologist. But seriously, people oppose it and will oppose it the night of the meeting because they are not true Americans, do not consider themselves Americans, have no loyalty to America, and notwithstanding what they take from the country, actually despise the United States. And on top of that, there will be cowardly liberals who know it's true but are too fearful of being ostracized by the radical left. Those people will refuse to vote for my resolution and may not even show up. They'll be hiding under their beds at home rather than taking a stand."

Sure enough, what I had been told about Cummins was indeed true. Cummins had fancied herself a close pal of Pat Buchanan's because Pat had written a column supporting her at the time of the "rainbow" controversy, and I was quick to inform Pat that she had opposed me during my fight over multiculturalism and Martin Luther King, to which he expressed minor surprise. I doubt that he ever talked to the old lady about it. But there was no doubt that Cummins was smarting over the flack she received from local conservatives over her opposition to me. And this new superiority resolution was exactly what she didn't want or need.

Cummins had her closest friend on the board, the liberal extremist Linda Sansivieri, call me at home to ask me to postpone the vote indefinitely because the district would have to figure out the cost. After I stopped laughing, I responded, "Nice try," and told her that was obviously just a ridiculous ruse for Cummins and the others to avoid this issue. For posterity's sake, I put my response to Sansivieri in writing. My memo stated, "In response to your question I have no intention of withdrawing my resolution. The financial aspect of this resolution is irrelevant – whether there is 10 dollars or ten million dollars available is irrelevant. What is relevant is whether or not this school board has the fortitude to teach the children the obvious truth. This resolution is self-explanatory and I look forward to implementing this mandate."

The day before the public meeting, the board received a letter from Chancellor Ramon Cortines, which board president Mary Crowley read aloud at the meeting. The letter was written in such a confused manner that it seemed as if it should have come with a ransom note. It was incoherent, factually inaccurate and internally inconsistent.

It stated, "It has come to my attention that Mr. Frank Borzellieri, a member of Community School Board 24 is attempting to place the attached resolution on the agenda... Frankly, it is hard to know precisely where to begin in addressing this resolution. I am second to none in my appreciation for our nation and its culture, yet I firmly believe it is possible to gain an appreciation of American culture and values without derogating other cultures, many of which have contributed greatly to our own. Moreover, one of the principles that has made this culture so great is its tradition of tolerance and respect for others. This resolution seems entirely at odds with that basic tenet.

"Furthermore, I am puzzled, because it seems impossible to reconcile this resolution with District 24's own multi-cultural education program. This program has as its very first stated goal 'to enhance the self-worth and self-esteem of all students by respecting each other's heritage, language, religion and physically challenging conditions.' Surely, the proposed resolution will undermine that goal, a matter I believe to be particularly problematic in a district as ethnically and culturally diverse as yours.

"You should also be aware that central Board of Education policy commits the school system to developing 'an appreciation and understanding of the heritage of students' and staff's own ethnic, racial, cultural and linguistic groups.'

"This proposed resolution is unacceptable and violative of both District 24's multi-cultural policy and the Central Board of Education's policy on multi-cultural education and promotion of positive intergroup relations. Neither Community School Board 24 nor any other school board may act in blatant contravention of central Board policy.

"Should your Board pass this resolution, I will immediately direct your Board to rescind this resolution, and if you fail to do so, rest assured that I will use all the authority vested in me to make certain that the students in District 24 receive an education which provides them with an understanding and appreciation of many cultures and which fosters inter-group understanding and awareness.

"At a time when we are embracing and welcoming so many new Americans to our school system, this resolution suggests that they leave their culture outside the schoolhouse doors. This is not what I am about, this is not what this school system is about, and I suggest you and other members of Community School Board 24 use this as an opportunity to demonstrate that this is not what your Board is about either."

Clearly, in addition to demonstrating his profound ignorance and anti-Americanism, Cortines worked himself into a lather for no reason. Nowhere in the resolution did I derogate other cultures. I would have been happy to do that in a separate resolution, with a keen eye on cultures that practice female genital mutilation, infant sacrifice, and those that force women to wear burquas. (Oops, I forgot, all cultures are equal.) He also actually appeared to be fearful that the board would go along with me. He needn't have worried.

In that day's edition of Newsday, Crowley had been quoted saying she hoped I would withdraw the resolution. Perhaps reading Cortines' letter was also a not-so-subtle nudge that I should withdraw it. Cummins, as expected, was a no-show, so we had an eight-member board in attendance and, as expected, a full crowd. After Crowley read the letter, she said, "I as the school board president do not want this resolution put on the agenda." Then it was my turn to put forth my resolution or table it. I said, "I have no intention of withdrawing this resolution. Board members will be forced to take a stand either by voting or refusing to vote. A refusal

to vote, as everyone knows, is the same as voting against."
When no one said anything, I read the resolution and moved it. Naturally, no one seconded the resolution, so it could not move forward with a discussion or vote. When the crowd erupted in cheers, Crowley said that the resolution violated the United States and New York's constitution because it "violates the concept that all men are created equal."

Excuse me, but the "all men are created equal concept" is nowhere near the Constitution. It comes from the Declaration of Independence. But what's a little inaccurate history lesson at a School Board 24 meeting?

Crowley later told Newsday and the Daily News that my resolution was "inflammatory, outrageous" and was "insulting to the many immigrants who lived in the southwestern and central Queens district."

This is actually my favorite argument that the liberals make because it is very revealing. Crowley and others who make it don't realize that they're talking out of both sides of their mouths and contradicting their own previous statements on these immigrants. In other words, when someone like me would remark that third world immigrants are not true Americans, don't embrace or care about American culture, have foreign loyalties, won't assimilate or learn the language, etc., the liberals recoil in horror. They counter that I'm all wrong, that we are a nation of immigrants, that these people are true blue Americans just like me, and how dare I say such an insulting thing, and on and on. This is the standard response.

But by saying my resolution is "insulting" to immigrants, Crowley is *admitting* that these immigrants' primary loyalty and affinity is toward a foreign land and culture, not America. If they were really the true blue American patriots liberals say they are, then the immigrants would be *flattered and complimented* by my resolution, since, according to Crowley, I would be praising *their* (American) culture. Of course, that's all laughable.

At that point in the meeting, I called the other board members "a disgrace" and "a bunch of cowards."

The next day's New York Times article, "Cultural Superiority in Curriculum Rejected," quoted Chan stating, "I'm glad it went this way, because it's a senseless resolution." The Queens Gazette quoted white liberal board member Jake LaSala stating, "There was no support for it at all. I just think he's off target. America is based on individual people's individual thoughts. You don't tell people what they should think."

I sure hope LaSala didn't raise his own kids that way. It certainly is the responsibility of adults in positions of authority to tell children the difference ("what to think") between right and wrong. I wonder, does LaSala tell his kids the histories of communism and freedom are equal? Does he leave it to his kids' discretion to decide if cheating and stealing are wrong, or does he instruct them properly? I wonder.

The United Federation of Teachers union (UFT) got into the act, too. In its newsletter, they wrote, "Clearly, when it comes to Frank Borzellieri's most recent test on American history, he received a failing grade on this report card."

The Queens Tribune wrote, "Many [board members] say they have tired of his campaign against multiculturalism and believe he is impeding the board from moving away from its Rainbow [curriculum] past."

Leftist white board member Elizabeth Gambino said, "I don't know what I should think about our board meetings anymore. I don't know where Frank Borzellieri is coming from, and I always wait for the next shoe to drop."

The next shoe would indeed drop when I would successfully reveal the hypocrisy of liberal board members who fought so relentlessly to keep anti-American multicultural books in the libraries and curriculum, but would fight even harder to keep pro-American books out.

Banning Pro-American Books

The liberals on the school board not only suffered from the disease of advanced liberalism, they also suffered from the condition of being unprincipled cowardly hypocrites. In no other issue was this more revealed than when I attempted to put pro-American, Eurocentric books into the schools and libraries.

In addition to all those afflictions, the liberals also suffered from advanced stupidity, as they didn't seem to realize how transparent and obvious their unprincipled cowardly hypocrisy was. If they possessed a modicum of intelligence, they would have cut their losses and supported my books, if for no other reason than to maintain some dignity. But they could not be swayed from the menace of left-wing political correctness, no matter how stupid it made them look. Even Norman Siegel of the New York Civil Liberties Union, who opposed my efforts to remove anti-American materials, couldn't believe it.

Since there was no chance of removing objectionable materials from the schools, I decided on a different strategy. I would propose *adding* books to the classrooms and libraries. Of course, I was lambasted by every liberal in New York when I proposed removing books, so you would think these open-minded folks would welcome *more* diversity of viewpoints, *more* materials, *more* books for students to examine in order to enrich themselves, *more* information… Think again.

At this point it would be instructive to review the two arguments put forward by my detractors in the multicultural books battle. First, their argument was that these anti-American books were just wonderful and belonged in the district on their own merits. But second – and this was the much more hypocritical argument – they argued *as a matter of principle* you simply cannot remove books from the shelves because you disagree with the ideological content; you must not censor books or ideas, and you absolutely must let children have as much access to information as possible in order to let students think for themselves. How profound.

(I am reminded of a local appearance I made before a civic organization in Glendale, Queens, soon after my widely-publicized battle against multicultural books. In front of a supportive and well-receiving crowd, I pointed out the two crucial aspects of my plan to remove anti-American books from the schools, lest I be thought of as a book burner of some kind. First, we're dealing with tax money. You have the right to buy objectionable materials with your own money, but not with the money of others. As an elected board member, I was a trustee and custodian of the public purse. But second, and more important, we are talking about very young children, aged 5 to 13. "How many of you would prevent your children those ages from looking at pornography, terrorist manuals, or even an obscene joke book by George Carlin?" I asked. Every hand went up. "Guess what. You're guilty of a form of censorship, of prohibiting children from getting information in order to make up their own minds. Are you crazy?" They were all applauding and laughing supportively. They got it.)

The press loved what I was doing because they love a good story, and this promised to be another circus. They even wanted a photo of me with my books, all lined up in a row.

I brought the books with me to the district office when board members were there for a working session. I told them I would leave the books there for all to take at their convenience and to look over. I said they could take them home or look at them in the office. In two weeks, I told them, I would be proposing we add the books to our district. Some board members took some books with them that night; others glanced through them in the office. No one said anything outstanding in front of me, but behind the scenes they were desperate and plotting.

These were the 15 books they would eventually ban from the district:

"America's British Culture" by Russell Kirk (Transaction Publishers, 1993)

"A Basic History of the United States", Volumes 1 through 5 by Clarence B. Carson (American Textbook Committee, 1983)

"The Battle of Lexington and Concord" by Neil Johnson (Four

Frank Borzellieri with the 15 pro-American books he tried to add to the classrooms and libraries of District 24, but which the school board banned.

Winds Press, 1992)

"A Children's Companion Guide to America's History: History and Government" by Catherine Millard (Horizon House Publishers, 1993)

"Christianity and the Constitution: The Faith of Our Founding Fathers" by John Eidsmoe (Baker Book House Company, 1987)

"Columbus & Cortez, Conquerors for Christ" by John Eidsmoe (Baker Book House Company, June 1992)

"Daniel Boone, Man of the Forests" by Carol Greene (Children's Press, 1990)

"A Documentary History of Religion in America to the Civil War" by Edwin S. Gaustad (William B. Eerdmans Publishing Company, 1982)

"A Documentary History of Religion in America Since 1865" by Edwin S. Gaustad (William B. Eerdmans Publishing Company, 1983)

"Founding Fathers: Brief Lives of the Framers of the United

States Constitution" by M. E. Bradford (University Press of Kansas, 1994)

"A History of Christianity in the United States and Canada" by Mark A. Noll (William B. Eerdmans Publishing Company, 1992)

"The Light and the Glory for Children: Discovering God's Plan for America from Christopher Columbus to George Washington" by Peter Marshall and David Manuel (Fleming H. Revell Company, 1992)

"Paul Revere's Ride" by Henry Wadsworth Longfellow (Dutton Children's Books, 1995)

"A Treasury of Children's Literature" (Houghton Mifflin Company, 1992)

"Washington" by Douglas Southall Freeman (Macmillan Publishing Company, 1992)

Taking board members at their word (or at least pretending to) as it applied to their notion that you cannot keep books out of the district simply because you disagree with the ideological content, I thought this was a great opportunity to see how much they meant it.

A Newsday article titled, "Queens Pol Pushes His Reading List," began "Frank Borzellieri, the Queens School Board member who sought to remove 'anti-American' books from school libraries, has now assembled a collection of 'pro-American' books he wants added to library shelves."

I was quoted, "These books are pro-American, Eurocentric, and for God and patriotism. They are truth-telling, and are not multicultural… The truth will be told. Columbus was not a terrorist, but the man who brought Christianity to the New World and was responsible for taming savage Indians. Founding Fathers like George Washington were guided by Christian principles and constructed the most successful and moral nation in human history."

The Daily News ran two articles. The first titled, "Book foe turns over a new leaf," stated, "Frank Borzellieri… still has literature on his mind. But instead of removing books from school libraries as he proposed last spring, this time he wants to put books on library shelves – but only ones he considers the right kind… Some of the books emphasize the role of Christianity in U.S. history. 'This is not promoting Christianity, merely teaching accurate history,' he said. 'Schools portray Columbus as a madman, but he brought Christianity to the New World.'"

The next Daily News article was more in-depth, actually quoting from one of my books and comparing it to a district book. It stated, "From 'Columbus & Cortez, Conquerors for Christ,': 'The reason many of us find history boring is we fail to see the sovereign hand of God at work as history unfolds...'

"By contrast, one history book being used in District 24, at Intermediate School 93 in Ridgewood, 'Exploring American History,' was examined by The News. The chapter on Columbus doesn't discuss the explorer's religion, and the section on slavery focuses on its brutality."

The Queens Gazette quoted me at length. "Borzellieri declared that the books he's talking about 'emphasize America's Christian history, patriotism and the positive role that the founding Europeans played in the formation of America... While the politically correct multiculturalists want to poison the minds of our children with this trash called multiculturalism – which focuses on every culture except the one that counts, the superior American culture, it is my intention to have truth-telling Eurocentric books placed in the schools.'"

I also appeared on the morning television news program, "Today in New York" with hosts Mary Civiello and Jane Hanson. With all my books arranged standing on a table, I discussed my proposal and New Yorkers got a nice clear view of this wonderful collection of books.

So I was certainly getting the message out, much to the anxiety of the other board members.

The New York Post had gotten wind of the scheme board members planned to use to thwart me and keep the books out of the district. It was the same information that had privately been passed along to me. The Post reported, "Board President Mary Crowley didn't return a call from The Post. But sources said the board plans to stop Borzellieri by forming a new committee to study new books."

The day of the meeting was a whirlwind of telephone calls in one direction – to me. First Cummins called me to tell me the complete lowdown on the nefarious scheme the board members had come up with. What Cummins told me was exactly what I had heard from other sources, but what is crucial to understand about Cummins as a source is that she was very close friends with these people. In fact, Cummins was called and told about the scheme on the assumption that she would be going along with it. The liberal extremist Linda Sansivieri, Cummins' close friend, called Cummins and explained that the board members realized they would look like hypocrites if they voted against placing books in the schools. So a scheme was devised by another left-winger, Elizabeth Gambino, to create a bogus "committee" that would be granted the authority to examine books and approve them before the board could place them in the schools. The beauty part of this scheme, Sansivieri told Cummins, was that not only would it put off the vote (allowing board members to claim the books had to pass muster with this "committee") but that a vote on these books could essentially be put off forever because the "committee" would never actually exist or meet. Brilliant.

This farce of a resolution reminded me of a situation which became a running point of amusement in New York regarding the sanitation department in the early 1970's. In order to get a job with the department, you were required to pass a specific civil service test. The problem was that they never actually gave the test, so you couldn't take it. If you couldn't take it, obviously you couldn't pass it. And if you couldn't pass it, you couldn't be hired. So the joke was if you wanted to be hired by the department, you had to take and pass a test that was never given! Well, this "committee" would work the same way. Books would have to pass through the "committee," but the "committee" would never meet or even exist, so books could never be added.

Cummins was absolutely furious when she called me. She had unbelievably harsh words for Gambino, calling her a "witch," and said Sansivieri was just "too damn liberal" for Cummins to convince her to switch sides.

"Frank, I want you to know I'm with you on this one. We'll go after them. We'll go after them," she repeated. "And Father Garkowski is with you on this one, too. I spoke to him before and he's very angry over what they're trying to do. We'll get them. Don't worry."

As you can imagine, having Cummins' support was a big mystery to me. Suddenly, she acted like my biggest advocate. Whether Cummins' support was the result of her having been sufficiently spanked by conservatives for having opposed me on multiculturalism and the American superiority resolution (the version I most believe), or whether she was sincere, I didn't know or care.

(Incredibly, I had done the Curtis Sliwa radio show this same week and Cummins called in while I was on the air. In announcing who was on the line, Sliwa, remembering quite accurately that Cummins had vocally opposed me many times before – and with the disco song "Ring My Bell" playing in the background – jokingly referred to Cummins as someone who had previously "rung my bell" and again wanted to "ring my bell" by opposing me, he assumed. Little did he know that Mary called in to support me. She got angry with Sliwa and challenged him to prove when she had ever opposed me, incredibly denying that she ever had. Sliwa, who is never at a loss for words, reacted as if the old lady was losing her mind right on the air. I let it go.)

Although Garkowski didn't call me himself, Cummins and he had been friends for many years and I believed her when she said he would support me. Although Garkowski's voting record was far too liberal for the community, and he was likewise far too intelligent to vote as badly as he normally did, he was not someone the other liberals would want to tangle with in a battle of wits. Gambino, Sansivieri, and LaSala were all intellectual lightweights, and Garkowski would eat them for breakfast in a battle of smarts, as I had always done. As it turned out, Sansivieri was the only one foolish enough to try and take him on.

I received numerous calls from the press that day, telling them what I knew and that we'd all have to wait to see what happened at the meeting that night.

Finally, Chancellor Ramon Cortines called. He was the only

chancellor I ever respected in my years on the board. He was always wrong and often logically confused but he had the courtesy to call me and try to privately dissuade me from my actions, no matter how convoluted his logic. He told me he had sent yet another letter to Crowley, told me what was in it, and faxed me a copy in advance. He kept harping on the fact that I called my Eurocentric point of view the "accurate" account of history and insisted that there was more than one point of view. I countered that I could not accept anti-American lies as equal with Eurocentric truth and would not change my resolution. We agreed to disagree and I went off to the meeting at IS 119 in Glendale.

To set the scene properly, I will describe how items on the board's agenda were listed procedurally. The first item would be Gambino's resolution creating the bogus "committee." The strategy of the schemers was that when that resolution passed, it would render my resolution not relevant because board members, by virtue of the creation of the new "committee," would claim that they would not have to vote up or down on admitting my specific books. But procedural nonsense aside, all that mattered was that everyone – most importantly the press and the public – knew that a vote for Gambino's resolution was a vote against my books. Obviously, when the Gambino resolution would eventually pass, I would still refuse to table my resolution.

In a familiar opening, Crowley began the whole fiasco by reading Cortines' letter aloud, which stated, "Once again, I find myself having to write to you about a resolution sponsored by a member of your board, Mr. Frank Borzellieri. The resolution seems to skirt rather than address issues of educational policy and to be a misuse of his role as a board member and policy maker.

"Instead of the previous proposal to ban certain books, this time Mr. Borzellieri proposes that your local board buy certain books which have a 'Eurocentric, pro-American emphasis,' which 'stress the Christian influence of the great explorers and the Founding Fathers,' and which will 'balance… the materials presently in the schools.' The resolution is offered in the stated belief that these books will provide the 'accurate account of American History.'

"No one has a greater love for this country, its traditions and its values than I do. Some of the books may well be appropriate for your district's schoolchildren. I myself very much like Longfellow's poem 'Paul Revere's Ride.' Nor am I in any way in my letter to you proposing censorship of particular books or ideas.

"But, really, this resolution is just a change in technique which results in the same end: repudiation of other cultures. The issue is not the list of books in the resolution, nor is it meant to be. The real issue is the language of the resolution and its intent. I am deeply concerned by the message it sends and its clear rejection of the value of many world cultures. As I have said to your board in the past, it is not necessary to derogate or ignore other cultures in order to celebrate the richness of the American heritage. This should be clear to all the members of the District 24 Board."

(I must interject here before concluding Cortines' letter. At the risk of using the same joke two chapters in a row, the letter really looked as if it should have come with a ransom note. It was so illogical and forced that I honestly believe that Cortines sat at his desk trying to come up with some reason – *anything* – that he could possibly use to oppose my resolution. He claims to not be "proposing censorship of particular books or ideas" but does that very thing by urging defeat of a straightforward resolution that would simply put books in the schools. He could have expressed regret at what he perceived my motives to be, and supported the resolution because the books were fine. At this point in Crowley's reading of the letter – specifically the part about "not proposing censorship" – Garkowski blurted out sarcastically, and with an incredulous look on his face, "No, not much!")

The letter concluded, "Our nation is a richer, more vibrant, more successful society because of the contributions of other cultures. It is for this reason that teaching about other cultures and recognition of their contributions to the American heritage is required by both central Board of Education policy and Community School District 24 written policy.

"Simply put, while some of the books mentioned in the resolution may well have merit, the underlying message of this resolution is at odds with these important policies.

"I am advised that your board recently adopted a method for approving textbooks for use in your district. This resolution, which seeks to purchase these books for the reasons he has stated, is not consistent with the process outlined by your board." [Well, that was not quite the policy yet, at least not for a few more minutes. I guess he was told the Gambino resolution had the votes.]

"Your community school district is a diverse one. Parents of many backgrounds send their children to the schools in your district. I would expect your board to use tonight's vote as an opportunity to demonstrate that Community School District 24 welcomes and celebrates the many different cultures and ethnic groups that are a part of your school community by opposing this measure."

Absolutely pathetic and shameful. Yeah, let's show third-worlders we will reject our own cultural heritage and cater to theirs in order to win their favor. No other self-respecting country on earth would do this. But indeed it was about to happen.

Elizabeth Gambino was a radical leftist who was endorsed in her election race for the school board by the Village Voice. For the handful of people not familiar with the newspaper, it is a radical liberal newspaper that makes the New York Times' editorial policy look like National Review's. It is a grotesquely pro-homosexual newspaper, with its main offices in the Greenwich Village section of Manhattan, a place with many homosexual enclaves. The paper regularly uses the most disgusting foul language in its pages and contains pornographic advertisements for, among other things, homosexual escorts and "dating." So during the subsequent public discussion, I continually referred to Gambino as "the Village Voice candidate."

Gambino then read her resolution, with the relevant part stating, "this School Board establish a policy... whereby a school committee, comprised of district staff, school librarian(s), teachers and the school Parents Association review all books prior to their being placed on school library and/or classroom library shelves..."

Garkowski was hopping mad for two reasons. First, he knew the resolution was simply a ploy to keep my books out of the district.

Banning Pro-American Books

And second, even on its own merits, the so-called "committee" policy would give unelected bureaucrats the authority to approve books, while leaving the elected school board entirely out of the process.

After Gambino's resolution was read and moved, the discussion – and the fireworks – began. Because of the many different speakers, I reprint directly from the public transcripts.

BORZELLIERI: "The resolution submitted and read by Mrs. Gambino, the Village Voice candidate for the school board…"

CROWLEY (interrupting): "What are you talking about, Frank?"

BORZELLIERI: "I was endorsed by the New York Post. She was endorsed by the Village Voice. What's the problem? The Village Voice candidate's resolution is a farce, designed solely for the purpose of torpedoing my resolution to add books to the schools. So after 25 years since the creation of District 24, all of a sudden the Village Voice candidate decides we need a resolution on library policy. Now I asked Mr. Quinn [the district superintendent] to research what is normally done to add books and Mr. Quinn did quite a bit of work, sent it to me and all the board members, and there was nothing stopping me from putting these books in our schools or having the board vote to put these books in the schools. Now if the board is against these books, they should vote them down. But to put this resolution on which is designed to even prevent the reading of my resolution is nothing more than political nonsense. Political cowardice has caused Mrs. Gambino, the Village Voice candidate, to write this resolution.

"Now if the Village Voice candidate wants a committee of unelected liberal education hacks to join with the UFT [United Federation of Teachers] who have already written an editorial against my books…"

CROWLEY (interrupting): "Excuse me, if you don't speak to the resolution…"

BORZELLIERI: "The committee is in the resolution. What is your problem, Mary?"

(Audience shouting interruptions.)

BORZELLIERI: "Mrs. Crowley, I request that I be able to make my case without interruption from the audience. This committee will be comprised of unelected bureaucrats. Why would you want a committee to usurp the power of an elected board?"

(More audience interruptions.)

CROWLEY: "Let Frank talk. Go ahead."

CUMMINS: "In the first place, I wish the audience would keep quiet until the board speaks, then they will have plenty of time to talk."

CROWLEY: "Alright, let Mrs. Cummins speak, but please speak to this resolution."

CUMMINS: "I am speaking to this resolution. I don't know the philosophy of the teachers in this school. I don't think the parents know the philosophy of the teachers. I don't know if they know their political leanings; I don't. Now suppose they recommend three Marxist books. Are we supposed to put them in? Would someone answer me?"

GAMBINO: "Mrs. Cummins, since this is my resolution…"

CUMMINS: "I am talking to the board."

CROWLEY: "Alright, excuse me. Elizabeth has the floor to answer Mrs. Cummins' question."

GAMBINO: "Mrs. Cummins, suppose this school board two years, three years down the road and this school board in the future doesn't agree with your perception…"

CUMMINS: "Of what?"

GAMBINO: "Of what's a proper book. I would rather see it in the hands of district supervisors, the administrators of the school, the parents, the professionals to make decisions for the children of this district… We are always saying let the educators do what the educators are supposed to do. That's what you say all the time, Mrs. Cummins."

CUMMINS: "I have never in my life said that. Never once, never once. So you're lying again. Now let me tell you this, Mrs. Gambino. I would suggest that you go back and read the decentralization law which gives this board the power over all curriculum."

SANSIVIERI: "We are policy makers, OK, and I think that is

what we are doing tonight, is setting, is making a policy here. We are putting books in libraries and I have a problem. Let's say for argument's sake we come up with four great books and District 24 rises tomorrow to put these terrific books into our library..."

CUMMINS: "Stick to the resolution. You told me to stick to the resolution..."

SANSIVIERI: 'What I am trying to say is we put fine books, any books and they were great books, and professionals in this district agreed... What happens down the road? It only takes five votes to put any books in our district, in our school library. They might be inappropriate, and I don't have a problem.

"This is a safeguard. I mean, we are an elected board, we are a lay board. I don't think we have the qualifications to put books in the libraries without special evaluation..."

GARKOWSKI (sarcastically, because there is no committee): "OK, Madame President or Mrs. Gambino, when was the last time this school committee met?"

GAMBINO: "Meet on a regular basis? I have no idea. Father, you would have to ask Mr. Quinn that. Meanwhile, I have set up..."

GARKOWSKI: "I'll ask Mr. Quinn if you don't know. Mr. Quinn, when was the last time – I'm asking a question of fact – when was the last time this type of school committee met?"

(Some back and forth inaudible squabbling.)

GARKOWSKI: "When was the last time, if anybody has any information, I would be very happy to receive it."

QUINN: "The books are reviewed by a recognized committee by central headquarters [central board of education, not District 24]. They draw people from the field to evaluate the books..."

GARKOWSKI: "Does this mean an elected member of this school board cannot recommend any books for our libraries? Mrs. Sansivieri said uneducated people on this board..."

SANSIVIERI: "No, I didn't say uneducated. I said incapable..."

GARKOWSKI: "Oh yes you did. Incapable? I feel I am capable of recommending many, many books. I am perfectly capable of recommending books for the schools. I have a BA, an

STD, an STL, an MA a PhD and a JB. I read plenty of books and I can recommend plenty of books and I am capable of doing that. Not only that, but I am an elected member of the community. I should have the power to say that."

SANSIVIERI: "OK, I didn't say you couldn't recommend and I didn't say you were uneducated. What I was saying..."

GARKOWSKI: "You said incapable. Do you want to take that language back?"

SANSIVIERI: "Excuse me. You can recommend, Father. But what I was saying was that there was some problem with five board members recommending books for the library, OK... I'm just saying I don't think it should just take five hands to say let's put these books in."

CUMMINS: "Where does it mention the board in this resolution?"

SANSIVIERI: "It doesn't. I don't think it does."

GARKOWSKI: "So the elected school board, the elected officials of this district are excluded?!"

LINDA McHALE (liberal parent from the audience): "Yes, I resent the fact that somebody would intimate that bureaucrats are unelected... There are books I wouldn't want on my kids' shelves in the library and I don't want to be told that my kids' library has to have these [Eurocentric] books because however many board members decide on it first."

BORZELLIERI: "When I wanted to remove books that were objectionable, you were against that, too, so why don't you at least be consistent? I see that certain books are more equal than others. If they represent Eurocentrism and are pro-American, then we have to keep them out, but when I pointed out the syllabus had a book praising Mao Tse-tung, not one of you opened your mouth to protest it, and I'm still waiting for you to protest it. But you have time to protest my books. Is anyone opposed to a book praising Mao-Tse-tung?"

(There was dead silence in the auditorium.)

CUMMINS: "The thing Frank is talking about was sent down to the chancellor, I think. It praised every holiday in the world except the Fourth of July."

After some more back and forth, the Gambino resolution to refer all books to the power of this "committee" was voted on. The roll call vote was six to three as follows: For – Louisa Chan, Mary Crowley, Elizabeth Gambino, Jake LaSala, Catherine Marlowe, Linda Sansivieri; Against – Frank Borzellieri, Mary Cummins, John Garkowski.

Now, Crowley wanted me to withdraw my resolution on adding the specific 15 books, but I refused. So the board had to take a vote to table it. Cummins protested that it was not legal for other board members to remove my resolution without my permission. It didn't really matter to me as long as they couldn't stifle further discussion, since my opponents were clearly making jackasses of themselves. So technically, this next vote was not on my resolution per se, but on a motion to table it. The roll call vote, therefore, was identical to the previous vote.

Garkowski said, "Well, before I cast my vote, I would like to say a few words. First, I disagreed with Mr. Borzellieri in the past for his untimely words and his bad decision, I thought [on the multicultural controversy.] But I believe, I recommend the actions of Mr. Borzellieri now because he forwards materials that he thinks are worthy of the children's education. He forwards it for our study, for our perusal, and for our discussion and for our vote. Now, the reason I brought up the other question [on the committee] is because I've been on the board for 18 years. In 18 years I didn't know there were any committee meetings on books going in our libraries. At least on this particular suggestion [my resolution], not only in this district but in other districts, a person stands forward and puts his name to a suggested list. I recommend these books; these are worthy to be put in our libraries. I recommend them. Does the community agree that the values here in these books are acceptable to the community? Therefore, I believe Mr. Borzellieri's procedure is a good procedure for publicly availing to the public an opportunity to study the books that are going into our libraries, so that whatever we vote on, whatever books we've voted upon, we've taken the responsibility for them."

Daniel and others followed the markers and rescued the girls. That was a great day.

Banned!
Ultra-liberal school board member Elizabeth Gambino objected to this image of Indians "dragging white girls into the woods" in the book, "Daniel Boone, Man of the Forests" and was successful in banning this pro-American book from District 24.

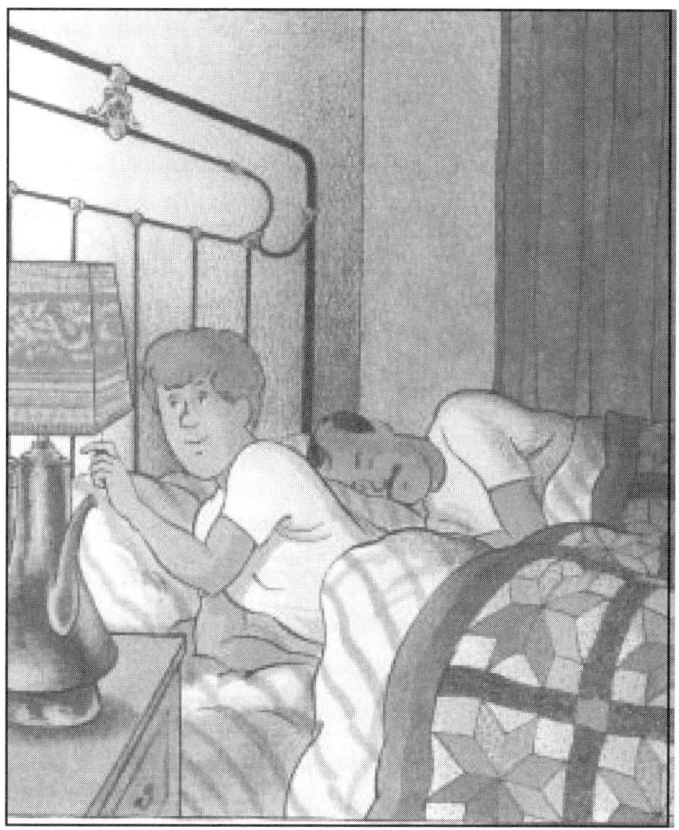

Wonderful!
But the same Elizabeth Gambino thinks this depiction of two homosexual men in bed from the children's book, "Daddy's Roommate" is just wonderful.

Cummins then said, amidst audience grumbling about Garkowski's words, "Stop it! You will all remember that I wrote a statement when Mr. Borzellieri wanted to take some multicultural books out of the library and I fought him on it. Now, am I going to not permit him to put some pro-American books in the schools?"

The audience interruptions got louder and more hostile, and Crowley was then threatening to rule Cummins out of order.

Cummins then finally said forcefully into her microphone, "You people are voting against pro-American books!"

What happened next couldn't have been more fortuitous for me if I had plotted it myself. Exhibiting stupidity beyond belief, Gambino then blurted out that my Daniel Boone book was inappropriate because it had a drawing of "Indians dragging white girls into the woods."

She was admitting publicly that she opposed the book for its ideological content – the very thing the liberals were pretending was not the case!

Chan, probably more out of liberal fervor than stupidity, then joined in. "There is too much Christian history and Christian values in these books. I am a Christian, but we also have to abide by American law, by the church and state. You can't just pull for one religion. You have to respect all the other choices."

What law, in heaven's name, was she talking about? Anyway, as Gambino and Chan were foolishly exposing the true motivation behind sabotaging my books, the other board members were dying. Crowley, anxious to move to the next item of business, tried to move on. But I made sure I got the last word. "Thanks," I said sarcastically, "for revealing your true motives, which everyone really knew all along. The voters will be very interested in hearing about this."

After the conclusion of the meeting, both in the auditorium and in the days following – just as had happened after the meeting of the battle over multicultural books – some people in attendance told me that though they didn't speak up, they agreed with me. Although I didn't say anything at the time, privately I had no respect for those people.

It goes without saying that before, during, and following this particular controversy, not one elected or public official – Republican or Democrat – spoke out in favor of placing my books in the schools.

Gambino later told the Times Newsweekly that "Native Americans" were depicted negatively in my book and that she also objected to my attempt to put "religion" in the schools.

The issue that the press was interested in after all this was whether or not I would submit my books to the "committee" for their review. Naturally, my response was that the "committee" would never meet and was never really intended to exist. (Years later, of course, I was proven correct on that.) I was quoted in the Queens Gazette calling board members "a bunch of hypocrites who are guilty of censorship."

I told the Daily News, "I will not subject my list to bogus committees of unelected, liberal, bureaucratic hacks."

It goes without saying that those 15 books never entered the classrooms or libraries of any of District 24's 30 schools.

The Bilingual Follies

Bilingual education is an issue that must initially be examined through two entirely separate lenses – as an educational program and then as a political matter. The political, as usual, eventually merges with the educational, and then swallows up the educational aspect in its entirety. In other words, years after bilingual education was proven to be an absolute disaster and educational failure, it survived solely because of racial and ethnic political activism.

Of all the disastrous forms of multi-lingualism in America, the most notorious is bilingual education. The calamity which began in the late 1960's as a $7.5 million program to teach Mexican children to speak English, has metastasized into a colossal behemoth costing American taxpayers billions of dollars annually. New York City alone spends half a billion a year on its roughly 150,000 bilingual-taught students. During my time on School Board 24, the district's bilingual ed budget was a staggering $18 million a year, which would have been better spent lining bird cages.

What started (theoretically) as a means to promote English among foreign pupils, has in reality become nothing more than a form of cultural rebellion for radical America-hating activists. Students, the theory went, would be taught regular subjects in their native language so as to not fall behind, while at the same time taught to speak English. When they sufficiently knew English, they could then continue their studies totally in English. But not only did bilingual education fail when that method was attempted, radical alienists are actually using it to promote Spanish among Hispanic children, *even if they only speak English.* One of the most common stories is that of Miguel Alvarado, whose 8-year old daughter was placed in a bilingual class simply because of her Hispanic surname. "We don't even speak Spanish at home," he said. This radical agenda is revealed more explicitly in the Los Angeles Unified School District's Bilingual Methodology Study Guide, which instructs teachers "not to encourage minority parents to switch to English in the home, but to encourage them to strongly promote development of the primary language."

The theory of bilingualism – which was to teach students in their so-called native language and English at the same time – has been thrown out the window. Bilingualism has in reality become monolingualism – only the native language is taught. According to radical Josue Gonzalez, director of bilingual education during the Carter administration, Spanish should no longer be regarded as a "foreign language." It should be, he says, "a second national language." At the annual conference of the National Association for Bilingual Education, many speakers actually challenged the idea of United States sovereignty by endorsing the formation of a separate nation in the American southwest called La Frontera. Mexican flags often adorn such gatherings. All of this should provide an accurate reflection of the mentality of rabid bilingualists.

What any of this has to do with life in District 24 is, well, in a word, everything. For the millions of dollars routinely and monolithically approved by the school board of this district were received, spent and wasted for reasons solely attributable to radical anti-American politics and activism. The white liberals were terrified at the thought of being labeled racists and they squandered their neighbors' hard-earned tax dollars to avoid that very privilege.

In New York City, the bilingual follies know no bounds. In recent decades, public school children have been taught in over 80 different languages! Some of the more well-known tongues include Kpelle, Nyanja, Twi, Gurma, Cham, Ga, Khowan, Bemba, Ibo, Oriya, and Ewe. No kidding.

The only fools who claim to still believe in bilingual education, in addition to cultural radicals, are the financial beneficiaries of the bilingual bureaucracy. People who make their living off the continued funding of a program are not going to admit the program doesn't work. Bilingual education has always operated under a sort of "reverse Darwinism," in Thomas Sowell's words – the survival of the unfittest. The more it fails, the more it is claimed to be needed. Every scientifically valid study has shown that immersion in English – allowing students to sink or swim in all-English classes – is the only method of effective learning of the English language.

Rosalie Pedalino Porter, the former director of bilingual education in Newton, Massachusetts, writes in her critique, "Forked Tongue: The Politics of Bilingual Education," "I felt that I was deliberately holding back the learning of English." Gail Fiber, an elementary school teacher with seven years experience in bilingual ed, said, "...I've never seen it done successfully. How can anyone learn English in school when they speak Spanish four hours a day?" Linda Chavez of the Center for Equal Opportunity reports that even tenured teachers have told her that "they do not speak out against bilingual education for fear of being labeled as racists."

The documentation of the failure of bilingual ed is so thorough that opposition largely cuts across ideological lines. Whenever a new study was reported in the press, the results were always that bilingualism was failing in its purported goal.

In some ways, support for bilingual education was even worse than for multiculturalism because the results of bilingual ed are tangible and can be quantified – just as a certain method of instruction in math can yield measurable results in students' math ability, so was the case with English proficiency on the part of students taking bilingual ed.

Unfortunately, there was no one as brave in District 24 as Rosalie Pedalino Porter – not district employees, and not, of course, school board members.

At school board meetings, I could cite facts on the failure of bilingualism til kingdom come, while cultural alien America-hating radicals could spout their venomous diatribes, and still the school board would always approve millions of dollars of tax money for this abomination.

Because District 24 was so well-known as the immigrant capital of the New York City school system, it was no wonder that bilingual education infested virtually every school in the district. Only the school board could have stopped it. But as usual, I was almost always all alone. In my entire eleven years on the board, not once was funding for bilingual education ever voted down.

It had been routine for the board to approve millions of dollars over the years without objections until I came along. Regarding one of the first resolutions to come before the board soon after my election, the Times Newsweekly reported, "Frank Borzellieri continued his one-man crusade against the City Board of Education's bilingual education curriculum by voting against a grant… [he] has been very vocal in his opposition."

But a big explosion occurred months later when the Board of Ed itself released a report critical of its own bilingual programs, pointing to poor results for students who had been in them. The report's release, which was front page news in the New York Times, caused a stir from radical alien groups. Naturally, I was waving the New York Times article around from the stage at the next board meeting.

The Times reported, "In a first step toward re-examining bilingual education in New York City, the Board of Education released a study yesterday concluding that the current efforts to educate tens of thousands of students in their native languages are flawed.

"The study found that students – even recent immigrants – who take most of their classes in English generally fare better academically than students in bilingual programs, where little English is spoken."

Chancellor Ramon Cortines said, "This report appears to show that our students in bilingual programs are not showing rapid enough progress in English language proficiency."

The Times article went on to examine the report in detail, but the main thrust was that the exhaustive research and quantifiable student scores revealed what bilingualism's detractors had been saying for years – that not only does bilingual education not succeed in the very objective that justifies its existence (teaching foreign-born students English proficiency), but that it actually has the exact opposite effect (prevents children from learning English.)

Now you would think that school board members would regard a report issued not by some national conservative think tank, but by the New York City Board of Education itself, as political cover for finally casting a responsible vote against squandering millions on a failed program. Think again.

A Daily News article, which appeared a day after the Times piece, focused on the radical anti-American reaction to the report. The News article began, "A Board of Education report that criticizes bi-lingual programs could accelerate anti-immigration fervor and cut back resources to foreign children, opponents charge.

"'It's all an anti-immigrant wave,' said Isaura Santiago, president of Hostos Community College in the Bronx. 'An ethnic backlash is always reflected in school policies.'"

The News continued, "Hispanic groups slammed the report for failing to consider socio-economic factors…"

I was quoted in the article, too. "However, one school board member said the study reinforces his belief that bi-lingual programs should be dropped. 'It's a disaster and a waste of taxpayers' dollars,' said Frank Borzellieri of School District 24. 'The way kids learn English is through immersion, the way my parents did in kindergarten. You throw them into a [regular] class.'"

At the next meeting, as I read aloud extensively from the Times article, I said, "Will this board continue to squander dollars of taxpayers in the face of overwhelming evidence?"

Chan, however, continued to maintain that the program was not a failure and spouted the tired cliché that "It [bilingual ed] should be a bridge not a crutch."

Elizabeth Gambino, in a rambling incoherent diatribe, said something about growing up with Austrians, Italians and Germans "without a teacher understanding their wants or needs." I've yet to meet any of those European-descended people she was talking about.

The resolution passed, with mine being the only voice of dissent.

On another occasion, the board was being asked to authorize $1,200 for the district's bilingual ed supervisor, Carlos Ledee, to attend a conference, the 24th annual of the National Association for Bilingual Education in Phoenix, Arizona. During the discussion phase, I wanted an explanation for this expenditure, so I questioned Ledee directly.

BORZELLIERI: "Is this a Marx Brothers reunion? It says this

is the 24th annual. I guess that means there were 23 others. What do you do, I mean, what exactly is accomplished at these things?"

LEDEE: "I am proud to represent District 24 in our conferences because District 24 represents the third largest bilingual population in New York City... When I go to a national conference, I go as a representative of the largest, most wonderful, bilingual populations. We network and share, we learn from each other."

BORZELLIERI: "Well, it says you'll learn 'strategies and techniques.' What can you possibly learn that you don't already know?"

LEDEE: "It works both ways. We don't just take, we also give. When we sit with others in those parts of the country that are a little bit further behind in their developmental program, when we sit together, we share our experiences, we share our insights, so it's not just a matter of take, it's a matter of give."

BORZELLIERI: "Yeah, I know. It's taking money from the taxpayers and giving to bureaucrats for weekend trips."

LEDEE: "I understand you just mentioned taxpayer dollars. My budget is 18 million dollars. I'm asking for $1,200 to attend this conference."

BORZELLIERI: "What difference does that make?"

LEDEE: "$1,200 from federal funds, which is .00001 percent of my credit. That's a small investment for what we get from it."

BORZELLIERI: "What do we get from it? Students who can't speak English and who are kept in the program for six years?"

CROWLEY: "Frank, OK, alright. Any other business?"

BORZELLIERI: "Now it says that there are nationally known experts at the conference. Who are they?"

LEDEE: "Well, then, at the moment I don't have the brochure."

BORZELLIERI: "Nationally known? Mr. Quinn?"

QUINN: "I can get you a copy of the brochure."

BORZELLIERI: "I guess they're not that well known if nobody knows who they are."

GAMBINO: "Maybe if you went you might know who they are."

CUMMINS: "Mr. Ledee, did I hear you say you had an 18 million dollar budget for bilingual education?"

LEDEE: "There is a total of 18 million dollars that covers the bilingual section... I can break it down."

CUMMINS: "No, don't bother breaking it down. The 18 million is enough to take my breath away without breaking it down."

CHAN: "I should also like to comment that the parents of these children are taxpayers, too. New immigrants who don't speak English are taxpayers, too..."

The resolution passed seven to two, with Cummins and me opposed.

The issue of bilingualism invariably would encompass larger social issues, such as English as the official language, the effects of immigration on the culture and the education system, and whether illegal immigrants should benefit from tax dollars.

As someone who had now gained a national reputation as a proponent of English as the official language of the United States, I was featured on ABC's "20/20" on a segment on official English.

Leading up to the broadcast, the local press ran stories on the fact that I would be on the show. Of course, I had already taped the show, so I knew what would be on it. Reporter Lynn Sherr and I took a stroll through Corona, a Queens neighborhood and part of District 24. No one spoke any English at all in the stores we entered randomly in the main shopping area. I joked on the show that my car had better not break down in this neighborhood. All of the magazines and store signs were also exclusively in Spanish.

In a different part of the show, I was in my apartment flashing official notices from the Board of Education in seven different languages, decrying this colossal waste of money.

Both the Queens Tribune and Queens Ledger ran stories on my upcoming appearance. As timing would have it, the newspaper articles would hit the stands on Thursday, the school board meeting would be that same night, and "20/20" would air the following night.

The Queens Tribune's headline read, "School Board Member on 20/20: 'Aliens Have Taken Over.'" The article began, "Controversial District 24 School Board member Frank Borzellieri stood alone in last year's vote to ban what he called 'anti-American' reading material from school libraries… Despite the overwhelming opposition of his own board, Borzellieri is undaunted in his quest to salvage the nation from what he perceives as the potential 'cultural ruin' posed by such literature and by the Board of Education's failure to extol America's cultural superiority in the elementary school curriculum.

"With those irons still in the fire, Borzellieri will be appearing on ABC's 20/20 this Friday… to discuss his stance on establishing English as the official language of the United States."

The article then quoted me at length. "Unless English is made the official language and unless multiculturalism in all its evil forms is eliminated, we will continue down the road to cultural ruin."

"[He was], the Tribune said, "… equating the ethnic makeup and condition of Corona with the occupation of a conquering nation."

I was quoted, "On Roosevelt Avenue I see flags of every Latin American country, blank expressions on the faces of store clerks when I ask for something in English, and even magazines like Reader's Digest totally written in Spanish… This incredible situation would have been no different if the United States had lost a war and been conquered by Mexico. Aliens have completely taken over."

On my fellow board members, I was quoted, "They're hypocrites because they claim to love multiculturalism. Except when it comes to their neighborhoods. They choose to live in lily-white areas. I don't see any of these white liberals living in the areas they claim to love… They're not representative of the community. I'm the top vote-getter on the board."

The article concluded, "With the unshakable belief he is pursuing the true wishes of his constituents, Borzellieri expressed confidence that his cause is correct, saying, 'In their hearts, people know I'm right.'"

The Queens Ledger quoted me speaking in a similar vein. "Absolutely no one speaks English here [Corona], not even the clerks in the stores. We may as well be in Latin America. We are witnessing the cultural ruin of America by a group of aliens who have no desire to assimilate into American society and no desire to learn the English language."

Naturally, I was welcomed that night at the board meeting with somewhat less than open arms. A letter had been received by the board office just before the meeting by someone named Enrique Lugo on the letterhead of something called "Instituto Nacional de Proteccion al Menor," although under his signature it said, "La comunidad de Corona Queens unida, la comunidad Latina unida."

At the meeting, Lugo showed up and read his letter aloud before the public and the board. I print it below in its entirety, word for word, leaving in all the grammatical mistakes and misplaced punctuation exactly as they were printed.

"Dear Mr Borzellieri :

"The fact that you sit today on the school Board of District 24 is a disgrace to this community, one of the most diverse and hard working community in Queens County whose achievements for a better quality of life for our neighborhoods, should set an example for others to follow.

"For you to come today as you have done in the past, using our children as pawns for your personal agenda is the last straw for your down fall. The fact that you refer to the Hispanic community as the cultural ruin of America by a group of aliens who have no desire to assimilate in to America's society an no desire to learn the English language, is proof enough that you are mentally retarded, a racist and an idiot whose knowledge of the American history is very limited. A country built on hard working immigrants from all nations, including Latinos from the true America's.

"Mr. Borzellieri you have no business in this community specially with our children whom you continue to insult and disgrace with your racial remarks. Take your person and your business elsewhere.

We demand your immediate resignation, if not we guarantee that you will not be able to conduct any business in District 24.

Get out ! or we will get you out !!!"

When Lugo finished, I took my microphone and said, "First of all, Mr. Lugo, I'm going to do you a big favor. I am inclined to take this letter to the police because there appears to be a veiled threat of violence and intimidation here. But I won't. I'm just going to throw it out.

"Secondly, I want to thank you for proving my point for me about alien cultures, right in front of the public and the press like this. Let me explain something to you about this little tradition we have in Western Civilization and American culture called the democratic process. You see, we have these things called elections, which legitimize my presence on this board because I am duly elected to this position by the voting public of District 24. I know this concept is foreign to you and you may be more familiar with military coups and other undemocratic ways of removing people from elected positions.

"It is not our cultural tradition to remove people from duly elected office by threats and intimidation. If that is the prevalent position in your community, then it does indeed contribute to the cultural ruin of American society by your mere presence here. The way we handle things when we don't like someone in office is we appeal to the voters, and at the time of the next election you galvanize like-minded people to vote me out, get yourself a crayon and circulate petitions, and attempt to have me defeated on election day."

Lugo was nodding his head arrogantly and defiantly. "Don't worry, I will," he replied.

I countered, "Well, I swear to you and to the public that I'll win. So we'll see what happens."

Once again, it goes without saying that no one on the board said a peep about Lugo's thuggish language.

After that meeting, I neither saw, nor heard from, nor heard anything about Enrique Lugo again. I did not, after careful consideration, throw his letter out. With the elections only a few months away, I photocopied his letter and sent it out as part of an election fundraising appeal. I also sent the exact same appeal to Lugo, so that he would know I was using his letter to my advantage. I knew the letter would be extremely effective in raising money when people saw the kind of threats I had to put up with. When I was re-elected by a landslide, I sent out a form letter of thanks to friends and supporters, including press clippings of my big win. Again, I sent this to Lugo also. I never heard anything from him.

Funding Illegal Aliens

In addition to bilingual education programs, the board also voted for monies for wacky alien social programs. One in particular jumped out at me as a subsidy for illegal aliens. Putting aside the fact that I voted against accepting all federal money as a violation of the U.S. Constitution, I'm speaking merely of the merits of this particular grant, which was for $379,811 and was labeled an "Emergency Immigrant Education Assistance allocation." I immediately wanted to know how many recipients of this money were illegal aliens. Both Carlos Ledee, the bilingual ed supervisor, and the superintendent Joe Quinn said they had no way of knowing whether students are legal or illegal and that there was no way the district could verify status. (Ledee obviously was upset at my constant use of the word "illegal"; he kept saying "undocumented" instead.)

"You're asking for money without asking if they're legal?" I asked. "There's no reason to assume they *are* legal, especially in this district. As a matter of fact, a high percentage of them are illegal. The money should not go to people who have broken our own laws. Instead we should use the money to deport them."

The exchange prompted the Glendale Register to headline its article, "Do Illegal Immigrants Deserve an Education? Question Debated at SB 24 Meeting."

The usual cultural aliens and white liberals went on about my lack of "compassion."

The Register article began, "...Frank Borzellieri... angered parents and teachers when he refused to vote in favor of funding two... programs on the grounds that such programs likely benefit the children of illegal immigrants."

The article continued, "Parents and teachers told Borzellieri to have more compassion."

One audience member said, "The parents are doing wrong so let's punish the child and deny the child the education? Let's not punish the child."

The Bilingual Follies

I responded to all this nonsense, "It's resolutions like this that encourage illegals to come here in the first place. When we're throwing tax dollars at people, that's an incentive to break the law and come here."

The resolution passed.

There are a few facts that need to be pointed out in order to illustrate the hypocrisy, cowardice, double standards, intellectual dishonesty, inconsistency, and general lack of principle on the part of school board members and liberals in the education establishment here. First of all, you cannot go five minutes in District 24 without hearing that we are the most overcrowded district in the city, out of 32 districts. If I heard the word "overcrowding" once, I heard it a thousand times. The world of District 24 was obsessed with overcrowding, with the need to relieve the overcrowding, and with contacting every federal, state and local official and their grandmothers for money, space, buildings, absolutely anything to alleviate this tremendous burden. Proposals were constantly on the table for more school sites, more space in available buildings, and so on.

At the same time, you could not go that same five minutes without hearing that District 24 was the most ethnically diverse district in the city, and had by far the highest influx and population of immigrants. (This particular fact was always spoken of as if it were a good thing – you know, the whole "cultural enrichment and diversity" crap.)

So we have two distinct statements of fact that everyone agrees on – District 24 is dangerously overcrowded, and District 24 has the highest number of immigrants.

Does anyone see a connection between the two? Ah, there's the rub.

Now, I can only speak confidently about people's attitudes in New York City, and specifically about District 24 (I don't know about the rest of the country), on the matter of new schools being built in the neighborhoods (or existing structures being converted into schools.) Those basic attitudes went like this: ordinary citizens who live in a community overwhelmingly oppose new schools in their neighborhoods for the following reasons – traffic congestion, noise, the presence of huge school buses, and outsiders being bused into the neighborhood. All of these concerns were believed to diminish the quality of life, hurt property values, and cause overall annoyance and aggravation. On the other hand, education and political insiders (those in the world of school boards) were fanatically in favor of new schools anywhere and everywhere, at all and any cost, and in a monolithic voice. The attitude was, "How can you be on a school board and be against more schools, especially in such an overcrowded district."

Well, there was of course, always a conflict between these two factions, and as a true representative of the community, I was the only school board member who ever opposed the construction of new schools, not only because I truly believed in it, but because it was important to represent the actual wishes of the community.

Now I must repeat that although school board meetings were technically "public" meetings in the legal sense that anyone who wished could attend, the reality was that only school board and political and education insiders ever really attended. That's why I was always standing alone on the issues at school board meetings with no support from the "public." Of course, at all other local meetings, such as at civic groups, property owners meetings and taxpayer associations, I was always well-received and popular. School board members were always notoriously uncomfortable at these gatherings because they were too cowardly to exhibit their true shrill left-wing leanings, until, that is, I would expose them.

So the next big issue coming up was the proposed new elementary school, a huge 900-seat facility on Grand Avenue, in the heart of Maspeth, a conservative white neighborhood in District 24. The School Construction Authority had proposed the site, where Staples, the office supply chain, was already planning to open a new store. The residents of Maspeth overwhelming wanted Staples, and this is the type of issue that will bring out people who never go to public meetings. But the hearing was not held at a school board meeting; it was held under the auspices of the local community board, which advises the city. School board members would certainly be attending and speaking in favor of building the school, but it was not an element they were comfortable in. Maspeth residents were angry and adamant. Some were openly stating that they didn't want outsiders bused into their neighborhood. Liberals reacted as if that were not a legitimate complaint.

When it was my turn to speak, I went to the microphone and read the following prepared statement:

"My position on this issue is pretty straightforward. Whenever you read about District 24, there are two things that you invariably find out. One: of 32 school districts in New York City, District 24 is the most overcrowded. And two: District 24 has the highest influx of immigrants. While anyone with even the most juvenile intellect should be able to grasp the correlation between these two facts, for some reason people choose to make the connection when they find it expedient, yet ignore it when they want to.

"If the city council, for example, was enacting policies that encouraged and invited illegal conversions [of one and two family houses into additional apartments – a hot issue in Queens – that added to congestion, fewer parking spaces, etc.] we would find it hypocritical and certainly a backwards form of logic to associate illegal conversions with overcrowding, complain about the overcrowding, and yet publicly endorse and even provide taxpayer funding for illegal conversions. Well, this form of upside down logic is exactly what this school district has done with regard to immigration.

"All we hear about is overcrowding, overcrowding. Well, my friends, the greatest cause of overcrowding is the obscene level of immigration to this district – both legal and illegal. Now if you are a reasonable and open-minded and fair person of even the most minimal ability to perform simple math, you will acknowledge the obvious – that there is indeed a correlation, a most significant correlation – between the massive immigration that this district endures and the overcrowding.

"Yet what has the school board done about this terrible problem of immigration? What messages have we sent, what initiatives have we taken? What have we asked of our federal officials and even local officials who have influence on them? Just as we are now hearing calls to contact our congressmen for federal money for school sites, what about our intentions to ask our congressmen to do something about immigration, since immigration policy is under federal jurisdiction? And finally, what actions has the school board taken which is within our own authority?

"Well, the school board has authorized, time and again, year after year, tens of millions of dollars for so-called immigrant programs which provide special resources, extra teachers – often imported – and a myriad of other things to cater to the specific needs of aliens. I will also mention the most disgraceful allocation of all – bilingual education. This has been done, of course, over my objections and my dissenting vote.

"Let's be realistic. When people see that this district is allocating these funds, it only invites more immigrants, both legal and illegal. Why should we be shocked that we have such an influx when we continue to approve these programs? And when it came time to vote on these programs, and we were having public discussion before the actual vote, I questioned the administrators about whether the programs distinguish between legal and illegal immigrants. We don't. We give this money away to fund illegal immigrants. What does this say? Obviously, it invites more immigrants. It rewards lawbreaking. It tells aliens who willfully break American law that if they break the law, not only will District 24 not turn them away, we will provide money and programs for them at taxpayer expense. Should that be the consequence of law-breaking – to receive taxpayer largesse? What signal does that send? When they see that we foolishly approve these programs, of course they will continue to come here, both legally and illegally.

"Had school board members, district administrators, and people on the inside spoken as vocally about this aspect of overcrowding, which is really the only one that matters, at least there would be some consistency, in addition to the fact that the real problem would be getting addressed. I get a laugh watching people feign such passion about our overcrowding problem, about the need for more space, about the need for more sites, about the need to twist the arms and lobby our elected officials for all these things, while at the same time not only ignore the issue of immigration, but cast public votes and voice support for the very policies – at taxpayer expense – that are causing this great problem.

"Let my statement tonight serve, therefore, as a wake-up call of sorts to the real cause and the real problem. People who think my views on immigration are not the majority view of the residents of Maspeth are kidding themselves. And besides, this is not merely a philosophical or ideological question on immigration. We have a serious problem and we must address it. Stop calling federal officials for help if you refuse to tell them to work to restore some sanity to our disastrous immigration policies, which are driving us to ruin.

"It seems more than disingenuous for advocates to bellow and wail about the need for more sites and more schools, and have the same people fail to recognize or address the main cause, the main reason we need more sites. The majority view in the immediate area of the Edwards site [for the school] is that it is a shopping area, and residents don't want a school there. That is the view I take, not only because it is my true belief, but because I am compelled as an elected representative of the area.

"There are some who believe that a school board member has an obligation to blindly support this site as a school. This is nonsense. We are elected by the community, by the taxpayers at large, not just by a handful of insiders. I am attempting here to represent the view of the majority of residents. Let our decision not only affect the Edwards site in Maspeth, but let it be a crucial message I'd like to send regarding immigration for the future.

"There are other sites not directly in the midst of a shopping strip, and we should maybe take a look at one of those. Thank you."

When I finished, the resounding applause and cheers in the room was so loud and heartfelt that residents would have been swinging from the rafters if there had actually been rafters. School board members sat quietly like the cowards they were, suddenly having lost all that courage they usually have in attacking me regularly in the friendly confines of school board meetings.

The events at the meeting did not go over well with one politically correct local newspaper. The Ridgewood Ledger, which was not a true Ridgewood newspaper (my home neighborhood), and whose offices were located in a different part of Queens outside District 24, wrote an angry and hysterical editorial titled, "When Bigots Roar." It began, "Just days before the dawning of the 21st century, a shameful display of bigotry at a public hearing in Maspeth showed that the lessons of the last century have eluded some residents of Queens. These Archie Bunker clones opposed the building of a new public school on Grand Avenue because they 'don't want children from other neighborhoods.'

"One resident screamed, 'We don't want 'em. Keep 'em over there!'"

The Ridgewood Ledger, the noble benefactor of children, telling Maspeth how it should think, stated, "The argument offered at the meeting by some that the school will increase traffic in this part of Maspeth is nothing but a smokescreen. The real reason for the impassioned opposition to the school is rooted in racism and xenophobia. The Bunkerites are afraid that the district will bus in children of color and children of newly arrived immigrant families.

"One woman… asked, 'Where do these children come from?' Another chimed in, 'these children will not represent Maspeth.' But it was school board member Frank Borzellieri, who went directly to the heart of the matter when he said, 'We are being swamped with immigration in this district.' We want to remind Frank that there were no Borzellieris on the Mayflower. [Where have I heard that before?] And there were none to welcome the ship."

I guess this rag was giving me some sort of backhanded compliment, in that I simply voiced out loud what all these other awful residents were thinking. I have heard that before, too.

In the end, the school board, as expected, voted in favor of the school. It stands on Grand Avenue today.

Ebonics

And speaking of "languages" other than English, it was inevitable that the most bizarre phenomenon of "ebonics" would finally rear its ugly head. While I did manage to get ebonics banned from the district, in a "pre-emptive strike" resolution (on the assumption that once even the strangest concept gains traction somewhere, it usually spreads elsewhere) it is instructive to examine this particular journey.

The word "ebonics", which is a combination of "ebony" and "phonics" and is more commonly known as "Black English," is a slang spoken by some blacks in America, mostly children and teenagers. It has been claimed that ebonics is a kind of dialect originally of poor Southern blacks who then imported it to urban ghettos. It has also been claimed that ebonics is traceable to African languages that slaves brought to the United States. Wherever and however it originated, there is no doubt that ebonics is a black cultural phenomenon. It is spoken exclusively by blacks born and raised in the United States.

Ebonics is easily identifiable upon hearing it. The average American, without realizing that it actually has a name, would immediately recognize it as black slang. Perhaps its most distinguishing feature is the lack of conjugating verbs, especially the verb "to be." Instead of saying, "What train are you taking later?" it would be "What train you be taking later?" It also features heavy slang and deliberate mispronunciations and misspellings of words.

The idea that ebonics is a distinct language is, of course, preposterous. It doesn't even qualify as a dialect like Southern speaking or even Brooklynese. Ebonics is either simply a moronic way of speaking, or more likely, the way a person speaks who intentionally wants to sound like a moron. The notion that ebonics is anything other than atrocious grammar is something that can only be put forth by cultural radicals.

Of course, that is exactly what happened.

The genesis of my resolution was actually an Associated Press article that spread worldwide in no time. The school board of Oakland, California declared ebonics an official "second language." Teachers were instructed that they needed to "respect its use" in the classroom. The district, which was 53 percent black, was the first in America to recognize ebonics as an official language. While some observers believed in the cynical view that the Oakland board may have done this simply to qualify for a ton of federal funds through bilingual education (and there may have been some truth to that), the reality was that cultural radicals were yet again imposing a policy that was pure insanity.

Oakland school board member Toni Cook said, "Whatever we are using now is not working. In my day, they would teach you how to talk like the white folks. Because someone says 'I be' does not mean someone is intellectually deficient."

Maybe not. But in this day and age a person who says "I be" probably has a cultural or peer pressure desire to sound like an idiot, much the way rap singers use misspellings, mispronunciations and general word abusage.

When the news broke, I was contacted by reporters. Very quickly I came up with a proposed resolution to assure that ebonics would never be recognized in District 24. Cynics who claimed I was overreacting, that ebonics could never gain traction here, and who simply wanted to avoid the issue and avoid offending black radicals, were either lying or were hopelessly naïve. History – especially recent history – has shown that ideas that seem outlandish today, when they eventually gain traction somewhere, pick up a momentum all their own. Think of the reparations for slavery movement, not to mention the recognition of homosexual marriage. With that in mind, I wanted to make District 24 the first in the country to officially ban ebonics.

Sure enough, while many people spoke out against ebonics, including Rudy Crew, the black chancellor of the New York City school system, there were proponents of ebonics organizing right here in New York.

While the California Department of Education sponsored a statewide symposium, Medgar Evers College in Brooklyn hosted a national symposium on ebonics.

Even an Australian newspaper, The Australian, contacted me for a very comprehensive view of the issue.

The article, which pointed out that ebonics was as much a referendum on black culture as on claiming it as a true language, quoted conservative black author Shelby Steele, who said, "Ebonics directs us away from the problem – the poor academic performance of black children – by emphasizing self-esteem and weak racial identity as the root causes of the problem... In the interest of protecting black children from racial shame, ebonics makes broken English the equivalent of standard English... We no longer have students with academic deficits, we have racial victims, identity victims."

The article continued, "Frank Borzellieri... is more blunt. 'Ebonics is an absurdity. It is nothing more than atrocious grammar and the decimation of the English language... Those people who support the use of ebonics in the classroom are just contributing to the incompetence and illiteracy of the people who speak it. The tragic thing is that in this era of political correctness, there is an enormous amount of pressure to accept this sort of thing, when deep down they know it's baloney."

Indeed, it was unrestrained multiculturalism, which had clearly gone mad, that produced this sick mutation called "ebonics." An "ebonics movement" formed in New York comprised of some of the most peculiar characters imaginable. It was a natural outgrowth of the absurd educational trends of the time, which recognize all cultures, languages and habits as deserving a place in public education.

The media buildup to the night of the vote on my resolution banning ebonics in District 24 did not indicate any opposition from any of the board members. The news just stated my desire to ban ebonics before it picked up any more momentum in New York. But privately, sources were telling me of two reactions being expressed by other board members. First, as usual, they hated the fact that it would be political suicide to go against me on this and they resented that I put them in this position. And second, they were concerned with offending the radical left by totally going along with my harsh wording. They would attempt to soften it.

Frankly, I thought that was a meaningless and transparent gesture, but as long as the only thing that mattered passed – the banning of ebonics in the district – I didn't mind changing the rhetoric. Sure enough, that's what happened.

Interestingly (but predictably), no school board member made a public statement criticizing ebonics. Perry Buckley (this was five months before he was to murder his girlfriend), the only elected black member of the board, did state publicly that the language of my resolution need not be so harsh. I happily took out my pen and took suggestions from board members and finally rewrote and read the final version.

One audience member told me later that I looked like I could hardly contain my "glee." Since it was so infrequent that I could actually get one of my proposals passed, she was probably right. Board members were dying to get the vote over with. Kathy Masi blurted out impatiently at one point, "It's just a policy statement. Let's vote on it and let's go." It passed unanimously.

The final wording read, in part, "… School Board 24 rejects any recognition of 'ebonics' as a distinct and legitimate language… recognizes 'ebonics' as unacceptable grammar and the decimation of the English language."

The Times Newsweekly reported, "After the meeting, a triumphant Borzellieri said he backed his fellow board members into a corner on the issue, and would have embarrassed them in the court of public opinion if they opposed it."

Once again, the Queens Chronicle identified the resolution's sponsor as "the ultraconservative school board member…" without ever calling the others "ultraliberals." And once again, the Queens Ledger quoted unnamed sources as claiming I proposed this for "publicity," as if I had trouble getting press. What board members resented, I pointed out, was that they were forced to attach their names to my proposal and rather than just consider it the correct vote for the district, they saw it as a victory for me personally, which they couldn't stand.

Charles Barron of the New York pro-ebonics group was quoted in the Daily News calling the board's action "unsound." Thereafter, although no New York City school board recognized ebonics, neither did any reject it outright.

Reckless Liberal Spending

It would be unnecessarily long and tedious to document every single resolution that was the object of the reckless spending of the school board of District 24. So drunken with the impetus to spend taxpayer dollars on every conceivable thing, the board made the spending habits of the United States Congress look cautious and thrifty. It is almost a waste of time documenting the items the board threw millions of dollars at. The school board that once had this ridiculous reputation as "conservative," not only spent recklessly, but didn't even voice skepticism at the nonsense being presented before them. If they saw dollar signs, they approved it. Who cares that it was their neighbors' money?

"Self-esteem" programs, phony "staff development", vacations, outcome-based education, even magazine subscriptions were approved without protest or even questions – not to mention, of course, the massive funding of multicultural, bilingual and pro-homosexual garbage. It didn't matter if a proposal had nothing to do with education. If it was proposed and contained money, it was approved. When I finally got on the board, although I would eventually be outvoted, at least the public got some sort of idea what this irresponsible board was doing on its behalf. Even Garkowski, who would only oppose an initiative if it violated a moral code (usually on the "gay" issue), regularly voted for things he knew were ridiculous. As a matter of libertarian principle, I voted against all federal monies as a violation of the United States Constitution, which, by the way, school board members swear to uphold. But the votes were easy for me because I also always opposed the programs on their individual merits (I mean demerits.)

So rather than go through the details of every single resolution on which huge amounts of money were spent, and rather than document my specific opposition to each of them, suffice it to say that in my eleven years on School Board 24, *not one* resolution that involved spending tax dollars was ever defeated. Except for one time – and although I managed to defeat the resolution, it was eventually passed a month later. So I managed to hold it up for a month rather than defeat it permanently.

The way I managed to do this was actually quite simple. On the nine-member board, five votes comprise a majority, so the world revolves around five votes. But a key rule is that even if some board members are absent for the public vote, five votes are still needed. It is not a majority of board members present that matters, but a majority of the board as a whole. For example, if two board members were absent, that would leave seven present. But it would not be a majority of those seven – four votes – needed to pass a resolution. The number would still be five. In fact, if only five members were present, a unanimous five-person vote would be required.

On this particular night, I already sensed an opportunity when I realized that three board members were either sick or still on vacation. This was the public meeting in late August, just before the school year begins, when the board passes about sixteen resolutions, some for about $20 million, in order to fund programs for the whole school year.

The resolutions were all very lengthy, consisting of wordy mumbo jumbo that no one really wants to read. Board members always rubber-stamped this stuff anyway, so there was no need, they thought, to be concerned about anything. On the other hand, I spent a few days going over every line of the resolutions and was ready to ask questions and demand explanations.

On those occasions when I did that, district employees who specialized in the given area pertaining to the resolution were asked to step forward and answer questions and explain things publicly.

When I realized that there were only six board members present, I knew I needed one more vote with me to defeat any or all of the resolutions. Cummins was my only chance. Although she had regularly voted to approve these types of resolutions every year, I still approached her and said, "Mary, just listen to my arguments before you vote." She agreed.

The first item on the agenda was something called Pupils with Compensatory Educational Needs (PCEN) for over $19.5 million. The supervisors for the district's department of "Funded Programs" stood before the board to answer my questions. PCEN contained a section called "Learning in Style." I began, "Please explain what this is about. I understand students at some schools are permitted to crawl up on ladders into little box-like areas in the back of classrooms to view lessons conducted by the teacher. What learning style would this be considered?"

I thought they were about to drop dead right there. They didn't contradict it.

"Well, there are different styles…" one supervisor started to say, without providing an answer.

Another question I had was, "What exactly are the holistic/global language activities?"

PCEN included funding for students' "regulating their own learning" and "evaluating their own progress."

I continued, "I thought the teacher was supposed to do this. If students are going to be able to regulate their own learning and evaluate it too, does the teacher simply provide the materials and sit in the back?"

Again, they had no answer.

I went on, "I want to direct you to another section which states students will be 'developing self-concept through activities that demonstrate individual strengths, interests and cultures.' What would be a cultural activity that would develop self-concept?"

As the supervisors were dying a slow death without any answers, I poured it on.

"Tell me," I said, "why are we spending millions on the whole language approach, which we know is a failure? Is it because reading scores are so low in this district? What's the difference between the Free Standing ESL [English as a Second Language] program and the regular ESL program?"

I then asked, "Why do tax dollars have to be spent to get parents involved in their kids' educations? Shouldn't they be doing that for nothing?"

No answers.

When Cummins jumped into the questioning, I knew I had it. She asked, "What in the world is a 'master teacher?'" When the answer was, "These teachers have a special expertise," Cummins shot back, "Who says? You can't throw titles around like this."

One supervisor admitted there was no objective method to calling someone a "master teacher."

The questioning went on and on, as I picked apart all 15 pages of the resolution, with Cummins joining in. When the vote was taken, there were four in favor, with Cummins and me opposed. Good-bye 19 and a half million! I found out later that this was the first time in history that a school board had rejected funding of this type and for this staggering an amount.

The district staff in attendance was numb. Rather than vile shouts of protest from the audience, it was as if more of a stunned silence hit them.

On to the next resolution, which was something called Quality Improvement Program Plan (QUIPP). The amount was $96,732 for "professional development." I started right in on Howard Weiner, the district's administrator for special education.

"All this money that's going for a weekend retreat for teachers, can't that be used to hire at least two more teachers?" I began. Again, there were no satisfactory answers. "Are spouses attending? Are there swimming pools? Saunas? Aren't these just party weekends that the taxpayers are funding?"

I continued, "Teachers are getting paid extra money to perform functions that should be performed by special ed supervisors and assistant principals. Why aren't they performing these functions?

"And why are we paying for subscriptions to journals?"

When Cummins jumped in again, Garkowski, who had been on the board with Cummins for some 18 years, asked her, "I don't understand. Aren't these the programs we've been approving every year?"

"So what?" Cummins shot back. "You are spending millions and I am looking at scores year after year and the scores don't improve."

After continued questioning from Cummins and me, a vote was taken and the result was the same, four to two.

At that point, right in the middle of the meeting, with 14 more resolutions to go, Garkowski, LaSala, and Sansivieri stood up and huddled together. Then they walked out of the meeting. At first I had no idea what was going on. Then I realized they did it on purpose because if the meeting lost its quorum, it could not continue. And Garkowski had essentially figured out that all of these resolutions were about to go up in smoke, so there was no point in continuing.

It was a huge victory. At that moment, I didn't know whether the resolution could ever be brought back for another vote when the full board was present. Unfortunately, it could, but it would be a month away and I figured I could use the time to get the message out.

I didn't have to try very hard. The press picked this up before I could do anything. The Daily News ran a story which began, "Two Queens school board members have held up receiving some $20 million in federal funds... because they object to government spending on what they call a failed school system and its programs."

I was quoted, "It's a big day for taxpayers. They're [other board members] a cowardly lot who think nothing of spending taxpayer dollars."

Cummins said, "They could throw money into New York City education until doomsday, but under the current system of education, it won't make a difference. Spending any more money is like throwing it down a rat hole. It's all this outcome-based education, where they concentrate on Johnny's self-esteem and they say no child is smarter than any other child. Meanwhile Johnny and Susie can't read."

An article in the Queens Tribune titled, "School Board Rejects Millions in 'Liberal' Funding," began, "In a vote that surprised many administrators, teacher and parents, controversial School Board 24 failed to pass two resolutions..."

Jeanne Pizzo, the district's director of federal programs, was beside herself. She was quoted, "They were programs that worked. I don't understand this vote and I don't know what the ramifications will be because this has never happened before."

Garkowski gave his take on why he and other board members walked out. "We finished because we weren't getting anything done. Mr. Borzellieri's arguments are correct, but whether I like it or not, we want the money in our district."

Chan was quoted, "This is a very irresponsible way of voting. How could they throw millions of dollars out the door? There may be waste in the education system, but this is not all inappropriate spending."

The article then stated, "But Borzellieri maintains that it is – especially in the case of the QUIPP grant [which] includes funding for such things as… workshops, a weekend retreat in November and materials to supplement workshop training for teachers."

My response was, "They call it staff development, but that means that the taxpayers are supposed to pay for these people's vacations [and] magazine subscriptions."

The supervisor Howard Weiner was quoted, "I have never heard of anybody turning down a QUIPP grant. If District 24 votes down this funding, we will be the only district in New York City that does not offer staff development."

Radio host Jay Diamond invited me back on his show. "Hey Frank, I agreed with those votes. Congratulations. Great job." I then used the opportunity to reveal that these types of programs are the exact nonsense that District 24 passes regularly, month after month, year after year.

The uproar over defeating this funding soon turned into a panic as the news spread around the city. An ultra-left-wing New York State senator named Leonard Stavisky, who had a special interest as a member of the senate education committee, distributed a letter to the press, which he proceeded to read a month later at the next school board meeting.

At that point, there was no doubt the resolutions would pass because the absent board members were now present. I had hoped that it was a one-shot deal, but that was not the case because there was still almost an entire school year to go and it was only mid-September.

Nevertheless, Stavisky started, "I am asking the members of Community School Board 24 to right a wrong that occurred at your last meeting." He then went on for two paragraphs about how essential the money was, what great things would be done with it, etc. Then he read, "If there are some board members who are not prepared to lead, then these individuals could make a major contribution to education by leaving it... At least one member of this board has already brought discredit upon this district through a bizarre attempt at ill-conceived censorship of acknowledged literary classics."

A literary classic?

I then blurted out, "I didn't know 'Jambo Means Hello' was a literary classic!"

Stavisky took offense and belligerently looked at me, deviated from his script and said he wouldn't yield the floor "to someone who does need an education. Don't demean public education because you have a perverted sense of hostility to it."

These two resolutions, as well as the others, finally passed over the same objections. The key thing about this episode was that it was perfectly indicative of all the resolutions that passed during my eleven years on the board, with only my voice as a protest. Though I got Cummins to join in this particular episode, she retired soon after and the same nonsense passed year after year. Although I publicly made objections to every resolution every year in order to expose the board's reckless spending, the monies were approved 100 percent of the time.

Homosexual Encroachment

"Frank Borzellieri has become Public Enemy No. 1 in the gay community." – Sarah Kershaw, Newsday, December 13, 1998.

In the chapter, "The Myth of District 24," I explained how the District 24 school board acquired the undeserved reputation as "conservative." That the district had become famous for its opposition to the radically perverse "rainbow" curriculum only served to surprise the public when the school board acquiesced to so many of the radical homosexual movement's demands in the immediate subsequent years. The individual members of the board were virtually all left-wing, virtually all of the time, as their voting records and public statements demonstrated. In fact, as I have already explained, the opposition to "rainbow" was in reality solely the work of Mary Cummins and John Garkowski, with the other members tagging along for political reasons. Once the controversy became famously public and voters in the district's conservative neighborhoods overwhelmingly supported opposition to the outrageous "rainbow" curriculum, the liberal board members just silently and reluctantly went along.

With all of this as a backdrop, many people might have been surprised at School Board 24's acquiescence and buckling under to homosexual influence, but they shouldn't have been. Unlike the multicultural controversies I had become embroiled in, where I was completely outnumbered on the board and lost every vote, I was actually able to obtain some small victories on the "gay" issue. Certainly, the motivations of board members voting with me (in the few instances they did) were purely self-serving, political, and hypocritical. But I was happy to take the win despite their cowardly reasonings. In the end, all that mattered to me was winning the vote. Nonetheless, this conservative "pro-family" image the board enjoyed because of "rainbow" was truly a ridiculous canard.

Famous Four Words

After I joined the board, the controversial issue that applied specifically to District 24, as opposed to the entire city, was the matter of the infamous "four words." Back in 1987, which was five years before the "rainbow" controversy, School Board 24 banned in its sex education curriculum any mention of homosexuality, contraception, abortion and masturbation. Only Cummins and Garkowski were part of that board. As the impact of this resolution grew while society in general became more liberal and permissive, a degree of misinformation spread. Some people believed that any utterances of those four words were banned in our schools under any circumstances. Opponents of the resolution were quick to point out, however, that the four concepts were banned as *part of the sex ed curriculum*, not in general.

I was always amused by this distinction, as if using these words in front of children would ever be appropriate, even outside the curriculum. While the familiar argument against the ban was: "How can you possibly, in this day and age, have a sex ed curriculum and not allow those words to be used?", the reality was that of the four concepts, the ban on discussion of homosexuality was always the biggest point of contention. And that was because the homosexual lobby was the most vocal and powerful. Since homosexual activity cannot cause pregnancy, the radicals in the movement didn't seem overly concerned about abortion or contraception. Nor do I recall any protests from the masturbation lobby. But the homosexual lobby in Queens and in New York City at large was loud, in-your-face, and regrettably, largely influential.

The famous four words became an issue again because the State of New York mandates HIV/AIDS instruction for grades kindergarten through 12, as part of sex education, which is also mandated. Given that mandate, the New York City central Board of Education approved an HIV/AIDS curriculum guide that was submitted to the individual school districts in the city for review. The districts then had three choices: use the guide as is; make revisions in the guide and submit the revisions to the central board for approval;

or submit an alternate program for approval.

Board 24 formed a committee comprised of board members, parents, faculty, and administrators, virtually all of whom were left-wing. Although I oppose all forms of sex education – even those focusing solely on abstinence because sex discussion should be the exclusive province of parents, not the schools – we were required by regulation to implement something, so I proposed an abstinence program called Free Teens, and even had the director of the program give a presentation to the committee. Naturally, the committee rejected Free Teens on the hypocritical grounds that the cost would be prohibitive – this from a board which spent tens of millions of dollars recklessly on bilingual and multicultural nonsense programs.

The content of the HIV/AIDS guide was something from a pornographic horror movie. It contained information so monstrous that I prepared my own nine-page single-spaced response. The introduction of my response read in part, "Once again, the radical homosexual lobby has achieved one of its political victories by escaping blame for its most horrible legacy, AIDS. The anti-academic establishment is also celebrating the publication of yet another monument to the promotion of illegitimacy, sexually transmitted diseases, and rampant sexual activity by twelve year-olds. The gods of Political Correctness are not only producing more material far too explicit for students, but are engaging in more brainwashing and left-wing indoctrination. And condom-mania is running wild, complete with the so-called 'success rates' and demonstrations, too." I continued to take the guide apart page by page, line by line.

The educator Thomas Sowell has written that sex education is among "psycho-therapeutic activities [which have] flourished in the public schools – without any evidence of their effectiveness for their avowed purposes, and *even despite accumulating evidence of their counterproductive effects...*" (emphasis added.) And Sowell wrote this without having seen this guide!

In my analysis, I continued to focus on the homosexual lobby's role in bringing all this public attention on AIDS while at the same time managing to escape blame. I wrote, "...homosexuals have performed a rather remarkable feat with all this AIDS business. They have managed to focus all this attention and political muscle on AIDS, without taking the blame for its existence and horrible spread. Homosexual culpability in the transmission of AIDS is so outrageously total that to discuss AIDS and its transmission without pointing the finger almost exclusively at homosexual behavior is the new Big Lie." Yet ignore homosexual behavior is exactly what the guide did.

The guide was riddled with references to "behaviors that could put them [students] at risk for HIV infection" without the slightest mention that it is homosexual behavior, far and above any other, that is the culprit for spreading the disease. The guide also asked, "How do people 'catch' HIV?" The answer was provided in a contrived "scientific" manner, blaming "sexual intercourse" in general, without targeting homosexual sodomy. This theme that AIDS was "everyone's disease" and could be acquired "in many different ways" while never blaming homosexuals, appeared on virtually every page of the guide.

But the guide was also very specific in some of its lies. In a True and False section, a question asked, "Some people say that only gay and bisexual men are likely to be infected with HIV." The guide's answer: "False."

It went on to say, "Seventy-five percent of all infected people were exposed to the virus through unprotected heterosexual sexual intercourse." In reality, the Center for Disease Control reported at the time that two-thirds of cases worldwide were caused by homosexual or bisexual males. Another seventeen percent were caused by intravenous drug users. Another eight percent were caused by homosexual drug users. Only four percent were classified as heterosexual. And even that figure was deceptively high. Of the four percent of those classified as "heterosexual," about half had heterosexual contact with a person with AIDS, and the rest were merely assumed to be heterosexual because the transmission occurred in countries like Haiti and Central Africa, where heterosexual transmission was believed to play a major role.

The guide asked, "What are some things people do that

increase the risk of HIV infection?" Now, if ever there was a place where homosexual behavior was the obvious answer, this was it. But the guide only mentioned "sexual intercourse without a condom," needles, tattooing and drug use.

"Who are some of the people who have been unfairly 'blamed' for the AIDS epidemic?" the guide asked. Once again answering its own question, the guide stated, "Gay people, Africans, Haitians, hemophiliacs, etc." If "gay people" have been unfairly blamed for AIDS, then Karl Marx has been unfairly blamed for communism.

While only lip service was paid to abstinence by the guide, its explicit language would have made a truck driver blush. And remember, this was to be the teaching tool for primary school children. The guide regularly referred to "mouth-to-anus sex", "vaginal candida", "venereal warts", "preseminal fluid" and "masturbation." It also encouraged teachers to explain "one size fits all" condom demonstrations; and instructed, "Buy contraceptive foam or lubricant…"

While the guide was obsessed with the wonders of latex condoms, it also referred to foams, creams and jells that could "increase the condoms' effectiveness…"

"Same-sex attraction," the guide instructed, needs "an atmosphere of acceptance." It also assured, "…we are giving our young people the opportunity to live and love safely…"

What any of this had to do with prevention of disease was anyone's guess. What it was in reality was psychological brainwashing in political correctness.

Indeed, the guide was a perfect manifestation of what Thomas Sowell had written, "…the ostensible subject of special curriculum programs – drug education, sex education, etc. – occupies a minor part of textbooks or class time, while psychology and values are a major preoccupation. So-called 'sex education' courses and textbooks, for example, seldom involve a mere conveying of biological or medical information. Far more often the primary thrust is toward a *re-shaping of attitudes*, not only toward sex but also toward parents, toward society, and toward life."

Sure enough, the guide asked students to bring to class

"sexuality-related newspaper and magazine articles, advertisements, and anecdotes to promote discussion of sexual choices."

Well, it was obvious that I had my work cut out for me. The homosexual influence on the board was very strong. I knew the only way to influence the committee to tone down or eliminate the guide was not to appeal to them directly, which would have been pointless, but to go over their heads directly to the public in order to embarrass the committee into making changes. So I released my analysis of the guide to the media and discussed it at the board's public meetings.

Early on, I made an attempt to reject the HIV/AIDS curriculum guide outright, putting forth a resolution that required the board to start from scratch without the guide itself as a starting point. The vote was six to two, with only Garkowski voting with me. (By this time Cummins was retired.)

Two of my sources eventually told me something I had heard many times (on matters involving the "gay" issue, never on race or multiculturalism, because even some radical multiculturalists were not pro-gay, so board members did not fear the homosexuals as much.) I was told that members of the committee were trying to walk a tightrope by placating the homosexual lobby and, at the same time avoid being beaten over the head and exposed by me. So while they agreed to stress abstinence above all other methods of prevention, the move was on to rescind the resolution prohibiting use of the four words.

While the committee was preparing that decision, I wrote an internal memorandum to board president Mary Crowley, which stated in part, "Although a final decision has yet to be made regarding the pending HIV/AIDS curriculum guide, there is little doubt that the liberals who control this board and that so-called 'committee' of cultural heathens will succeed in ramming a pro-homosexual monstrosity down the throats of unsuspecting parents."

And as I prepared to take the battle to the press and public, the committee was indeed preparing to recommend to the full board the use of the words "condom" and "contraception." But this would be a tricky maneuver politically because first there was the annoying matter of the 1987 resolution banning the four words. Now to the casual observer, it might not appear to be that difficult of a deal. Simply rescind the 1987 resolution, then pass the new resolution for the new curriculum guide.

Ah, but that simple analysis does not take into consideration the political realities. Just as congress enacts pay raises in the middle of the night or buries them in some huge appropriations bill so the public won't notice, members of the board did not want to be seen in the community as voting for allowing the use of these words to primary and middle school children. Life would have been much easier if the resolution had not existed; they could simply approve the guide. And they knew I would make a public spectacle out of any effort to rescind the 1987 resolution.

It should further be explained that the resolution to ban the four words, had it never been passed in 1987, would never have passed when I was on the board. That is because politically there is a world of difference between being pro-active and *passing* a resolution to ban the four words, and *rescinding* a resolution which already exists. It is akin politically to a presidential candidate who, as a senator, voted against certain tax cuts. But once they were already law, he would not vote to rescind them. It's a total political mindset, and school board members on Board 24 were, of course, political animals, and spineless ones at that.

As the fight over the curriculum guide became citywide news, which included various television appearances by Chan and me, the Queens Chronicle, Queens Gazette, and Times Newsweekly went with front page stories.

Naturally, the Chronicle identified me as "the extremely conservative" Frank Borzellieri. (Chan, Sansivieri, and Masi were never identified as "extremely liberal," even though their voting records were the exact opposite of mine.) It also casually referred to my battle over multiculturalism as "his book burning proposal." I attribute the Chronicle's bias more to an institutional mindset at the paper than to any nefarious motives by the reporter, Betty Cooney. All of that notwithstanding, I was quoted accurately and at length.

"While Borzellieri doesn't deny he is 'opposed to sex education in principle'," the paper wrote, as if I might be trying to hide that fact.

"Although not a parent himself..." the Chronicle continued, restating a common theme in order to suggest that being childless means one does not possess one's common sense and moral compass.

And, "The Chronicle asked Borzellieri if his opposition was based on religious views. He said that it was 'more for moral reasons.'

"He said there were two major reasons he felt this way. The first is 'pragmatic. It doesn't work,' he explained. He noted that the sex education programs were introduced in the mid 70s to gain control of growing problems and to bring down the birth rates in unwed teens. 'It didn't bring down the rate. In fact it went up,' Borzellieri said.

"The second reason he explained is, 'it is not for the schools (to teach sex education), it is the job of the parents.'

"He claims that the new curriculum ... fails to blame 'homosexuals and the homosexual lifestyle' for the spread of AIDS."

The Gazette actually ran two front page stories within four issues. The first, in an article titled, "Borzellieri Adamant in Stance Against Sex Ed Curriculum", I was quoted, "I'm totally against it, from demonstrating the use of condoms to the explicit language for 10 and 11-year olds... Throughout the 215-page guide, there's not a single word to place the blame for the AIDS epidemic on homosexuals and the homosexual lifestyle, which is the main reason for the spread of AIDS. I say toss the whole thing out. Parents should be teaching sex education, not the schools."

The article went on, "Borzellieri, known for his extremely conservative views... while harping on the point that the true blame for the spread of HIV/AIDS rests with the homosexual community, Borzellieri is sharply critical of the creators of the curriculum, he said, for never stating this point in numerous instances, but instead resorting to half truths and deceptions."

In the subsequent article, the Gazette covered the board's discussion of the issue at its public meeting. "After an expression of opposing viewpoints, dominated by board member Frank Borzellieri's assertions that the proposed curriculum was inappropriate..." The Gazette also quoted me as criticizing the "screaming liberal committee."

The Times Newsweekly pointed out my skepticism about the committee's desire to be forthright and public about the work they had done. Reporter Paul Toomey wrote that, "Because of the late hour [Kathy] Masi [the chair of the committee] said she would not read the report on her Committee's HIV/AIDS Curriculum… but would make it available to those interested."

Since I insisted on discussing it so the public would know what was going on, the paper further wrote, "The conservative called the Central Board's curriculum guide a 'monstrous slap at traditional moral values' and a 'blatant promotion of promiscuity.'"

The Daily News quoted me as stating sarcastically, "One-third of our 17-year olds don't know that Lincoln wrote the Emancipation Proclamation. But they certainly know how to use a condom."

The importance of these articles was two-fold. They brought the issue exactly where I wanted it – to the public's attention and consciousness. And by presenting me as the aggressor, they revealed how truly uncomfortable and cowardly the other board members were in revealing their true beliefs on these matters (excepting Chan who was always forthright.)

All of this was coming to an Armageddon on the issue, with Chan moving aggressively to propose rescinding the district's ban on the four words. Her ideological allies were useless to her because they were too cowardly to stand up publicly for their true beliefs. So Chan and I were everywhere, being quoted in the press and debating on the morning television program Good Day New York.

Chan's resolution was on the agenda for that week's board meeting and the saturation coverage insured that the city was ready. Her resolution read, in part: "Resolved, that this school board hereby rescind that part of Resolution 28… that banned any reference to the topics of homosexuality, abortion, contraception, and masturbation in the Family Living Including Sex Education curriculum… This absolute policy is unrealistic and unduly constrains teachers from the discussion of ideas and attitudes that will help District 24's children develop into responsible, healthy adults."

So the very resolution itself contained language which Sowell warned of when he referred to sex ed's "primary thrust is toward a re-shaping of attitudes."

Newsday, although the most liberal paper in the city, had always given me the most fair and unbiased coverage. They did two major pieces on the upcoming showdown. The first article began with the ominous sentence, "No teacher employed by Community School District 24 in western Queens is permitted to read this article to students because it contains four words that have been censored from the curriculum and banned from classroom discussions: masturbation, homosexuality, abortion and contraception."

The piece quoted Rosemary Parker, a special education teacher in the district, complaining, "How do you teach about AIDS if you can't use the word contraception or condom?" Of course, the liberal mindset cannot conceive of a more common sense notion that you simply preach abstinence or don't discuss AIDS at all.

A longtime left-wing parent association president, Mary Lazaro, was also quoted. She told Newsday, "I grew up in the '60s, so personally, I don't think anything should be banned."

Great. So let's bring in pornography, which will really give the kids an education, not to mention sex toys, cucumbers, and lubricants, so they can get some genuine real-world experience.

Another liberal teacher in the district, Susan Picicci, said, "You deal with it, you live with the restrictions. We feel our hands are tied, but that's life in District 24."

But a parent named Dorothy Witkowski said, "Children under 11 shouldn't be taught that kind of stuff in school. They should ask their parents."

Newsday's other major piece featured a huge photo of Chan with her 13 year old daughter, Carolyn. Chan was quoted, "Like many parents bringing up children in these complex times, I find it awkward to discuss these topics with them."

Fine, so let's leave it in the hands of liberal educators, she says.

I was described in the article as "33, a childless bachelor who grew up attending a Catholic school…" I was quoted stating sex education "really promotes promiscuity."

The Times Newsweekly ran an article on the upcoming board

meeting which emphasized the enormous publicity the issue had received. "With a bevy of police and auxiliary police officers stationed in the vestibule of IS 119..." the article stated, indicating that a large contingent of homosexual protesters was expected.

Because elections were coming up, it was no surprise to me, nor to Chan herself, that her resolution would go nowhere. Before voting and public discussion on a resolution, the proposal must be seconded by a separate board member. When Chan read her resolution and received no second, it died right there. The liberals were too cowardly to vote their true beliefs or to even second the resolution, which would have opened it up for public discussion. While I considered it a victory nonetheless since the prohibition of the four words would remain in effect, in retrospect I might have seconded the resolution to force board members to at least vote, but at the risk of it passing I let well enough alone.

Chan exploded when no one would second her resolution. "Hiding a problem does not solve a problem!" she bellowed.

When reporters approached us after the meeting, I simply reiterated that the topics were an "abomination."

The most bizarre advocacy for rescinding the ban on the four words did not come from so-called "health" professionals, teachers, or Planned Parenthood types, but from the radical homosexual activists. While homosexual perversions have no connection to abortion, pregnancy or contraception, "gays" do have an interest in condoms and, of course, discussion of homosexuality. In an official complaint written to the district protesting the sex education policy, Daniel Dromm, the head of the Queens Lesbian and Gay Pride Committee and a teacher in the district, wrote, "By 'eliminating' homosexuality from the Family Living/Sex Education curriculum, District 24 is discriminating on the basis of sexual orientation in 'its programs.'"

Although Chan was defeated, and the ban on the four words was a firewall on any sex education curriculum, as time went on it became obvious that the genie could not be placed back in the bottle. Pressure continued to mount on board members to reverse the policy and there was discussion about getting around the precise letter of the 1987 resolution by discussing the four topics *outside* the sex ed curriculum, where discussion was technically not banned.

Daniel Dromm: The Queer of Queens

At this point, I should explain the continuing unfolding of the issue as it related to Daniel Dromm's activities. Dromm, a hysterical homosexual teacher in the district, was in the forefront of every controversy concerning the radical homosexual movement. In fact, in every public din involving homosexual perversion, there was Dromm right in the middle. Dromm first became an agitator when, he said, in response to the "rainbow" curriculum controversy, he "outed" himself to his fourth grade class, but there was much more to come.

Since my protracted and ongoing battles through the years with Dromm were the constant source of citywide news, it would be instructive to chronicle Dromm's antics in chronological order going back to 1992 in order to observe exactly what I was dealing with. Since my detractors always see fit to point out my beliefs, actions, and statements (which I don't mind – in fact, welcome – as long as they are accurate) it would also be instructive to reveal Dromm's background and beliefs.

Soon after my election to the board, Dromm revealed that he had "outed" himself to his class of fourth grade nine-year olds at PS 199 in Long Island City. In response to a political column by retired principal Howard Hurwitz which criticized radical homosexuals for "outing" other homosexuals who wished to keep their homosexuality private, Dromm, in a letter to the Times Newsweekly, wrote, "Horrible Howard Hurwitz' homophobic harangue helps homosexuals…. His [Hurwitz's] harangues helped galvanize our community like never before. I came out to my fourth grade class in response to Howard… [for his role in opposing the "rainbow" curriculum the year before.]"

So Dromm was now admitting publicly that he was discussing his homosexuality with his students.

To that point, I had never heard of Daniel Dromm. No sooner

had I been horrified to read Dromm's admission, Hurwitz wrote a letter to the board requesting that charges be leveled against Dromm for "conduct unbecoming a teacher." In a private letter to the editor of the Times Newsweekly, Hurwitz responded, "What saddens me, although I should be inured to sadness as I live through the decline in morality, is that Daniel P. Dromm, who told his class that he is a sexual pervert, will be returning [to school] in September."

Soon after, Hurwitz called me. We agreed that because of the political nature of the issue, it shouldn't be treated as just another personnel matter and that Cummins and I should push the issue. (As a matter of clarification, the school board did not usually get directly involved in personnel matters. The district superintendent generally handled personnel matters and, in some extreme cases, was required to bring the issue to the board in private closed sessions for a vote regarding discipline.)

At the very next public meeting of the board, I brandished a copy of the letter, promising disciplinary action of some kind. Cummins joined in, but the rest of the board sat silently. When Cummins and I pushed Superintendent Quinn, he responded calmly, "The matter is being looked into."

Although nothing was ever officially brought to the board, Dromm was brought to a disciplinary hearing by his principal, Jack Birbiglia. As reported in New York magazine, Dromm said, "I got a call from someone who'd attended a school board meeting. She told me that Cummins and Borzellieri were waving a copy of my letter and calling for disciplinary action against me."

New York magazine continued, "Sure enough, three days later, Dromm was called down to principal Jack Birbiglia's office for a formal disciplinary action." A union member was also present at the meeting and Birbiglia warned Dromm to never, according to New York magazine, "initiate discussions about his homosexuality, or to pursue, clarify, or moralize about the issue." According to Dromm, Birbiglia told him otherwise "the district would cut my balls off."

New York magazine also interviewed me and quoted me as stating, "To reveal one's perversion in front of 10-year-olds – that speaks for itself."

Dromm's problems with Birbiglia did not end there. At PS 199, Dromm posted a flyer in the faculty lounge about an activity sponsored by the Lesbian and Gay Teachers Association. Dromm said that Birbiglia tore it down, stating he had "little children to protect." An unnamed teacher at PS 199 told New York, "Is it really good to have this all out in the open? They're still babies. We're robbing these kids of their childhood."

In a telephone conversation I had with Birbiglia, he essentially corroborated those versions of events.

In response to the flyer incident, Dromm showed up at a public school board meeting and, railing against his supposed oppression, deliberately and defiantly placed a similar flyer on the wall. It was immediately removed by a security guard and Dromm was ruled out of order.

Dromm was also featured in a separate piece in Newsday. Dromm was complaining that the complaint he filed against Birbiglia with the city's Human Rights Commission was a loser. Their ruling on this "sexual orientation" complaint was that Dromm had not been discriminated against. In documenting Dromm's travails, Newsday then wrote, "All the while, an ultraconservative board member, Frank Borzellieri, has at various times called for Dromm's resignation." The article continued, "Dromm says he has the right to tell his students he is gay… children need to know, says Dromm, that it is OK to be gay."

Because of all this publicity, Dromm became sort of a go-to person on the part of the press on any issue concerning the radical homosexual lobby. I observed Dromm taping a public access talk show when I was also in the studio waiting to tape the following show. To no one's surprise, Dromm expressed support for both the 1972 Gay Rights Platform and the platform of the 1993 March on Washington for "Lesbian, Gay, and Bi Equal Rights and Liberation."

And just what exists on those platforms that Dromm and organized gaydom support and demand?

*Homosexual adoptions and the redefinition of the family: "We demand legislation to prevent discrimination against Lesbians, Gays,

Bisexuals and transgendered people in areas of family diversity, custody, adoption and foster care and that the definition of family includes the full diversity of all family structures."

*Homosexual polygamy: "Legalization of multiple partner unions."

*Lower age of sexual consent for children: "The implementation of laws that recognize sexual relationships among youth, between consenting peers."

*Medical insurance coverage for sex-change operations: "The redefinition of sexual re-assignment surgeries as medical, not cosmetic, treatment."

*Ban ROTC from campuses: "The ban of all discriminatory ROTC programs and recruiters from learning institutions."

*Admit AIDS-infected immigrants: "Repeal all discriminatory immigrant laws based on race and HIV status."

*Legalize homosexual marriages: "Recognition of domestic partnerships and legalization of same sex marriages."

*Force Boy Scouts to accept homosexuals: "An end to discrimination based on sexual orientation in all programs of the Boy Scouts of America."

As outrageously unseemly as Dromm's affinity for these demands is, there are two further points to make about him. The first is that *not one* elected official ever denounced Dromm, his actions, or his support of these positions. Whenever Dromm was mentioned by New York City officials, it was always an expression of support (and a demand that I leave him alone.)

But the second point about Dromm is his own grotesque background as a homosexual pervert. In a shocking article in Ripe Magazine titled, "Daniel Dromm, A Prince in Queer Queens," Dromm admitted that as a teenager he went to "tea rooms" (public bathrooms), where, he said, "I had my first gay experience." He revealed that he was arrested for a homosexual sex act in a Long Island parking lot. When brought to the police station he lied to the cops, telling them he did it for the money. Dromm pled guilty to solicitation and was remanded by the judge into psychiatric care.

Dromm said that when he was 18 he went to a dance at the Gay

Activist Alliance in Manhattan. He said, "I liked political action and fit in immediately with the alliance who were radical." He continued, "I had some really swishy friends and we used to all go to the disco together… I went to a Catholic college where I became a bit of a radical because I was very out… I was very effeminate, smoked lemon cigarettes and wore platform shoes."

In the article, Dromm chronicled his outspokenness about the "rainbow" curriculum and claimed, "It was a very positive reaction to my coming out." He said, "… we have to teach tolerance beginning in kindergarten." In other words, teach five year olds that homosexuality is normal.

He said, "Current school board member Frank Borzellieri is worse than Cummins. He doesn't believe in multiculturalism, is opposed to bilingual education, and does not want Martin Luther King taught in schools. He's an anti-gay, anti-immigrant, anti-African American equal opportunity hater, and threatened to knock Wayne's teeth down his throat" [referring to radical homosexual Wayne Mahlke, a pal of Dromm's who was running for the school board. This accusation against me was false, and Mahlke lost the election anyway.]

Dromm then went on to glow about the annual "Queens Lesbian and Gay Pride Parade and Festival," a disgusting annual display in Jackson Heights, Queens. "Families with children watch the parade," he said. "Kids from my school were there with their parents, as well as fellow teachers – people who I've seen year after year. They get such a kick out of the drag queens as they applaud them…"

He also admitted that three drag queens pulled their tops down and the police condemned the parade as "lewd."

He went on about his political activities. "There have been guys in the movement that I liked but it didn't work out and there's sexual things that happen but they're not relationships."

Some role model.

No kidding. In an article Dromm authored for the Queens Courier titled, "Why I'm an Out Gay Teacher," Dromm began, "It's important to me to be open about being gay in all areas of my life, and not only because I want to be honest. As a teacher, I want to be a positive role model for my students, especially to the ten percent or so who are growing up to be lesbian or gay."

He has also written, "Today as a gay man, I am committed to advancing the day when children will grow up believing that being lesbian, gay, bisexual or transgendered is a part of God's plan. I look around my classroom and I know that of the 34 kids I teach, at least three will grow up to be gay. Those youngsters need to know that gay is good because they are good."

So not only is Dromm, in his own mind, a positive role model (considering everything previously described), but he also wants to be honest. I must digress at this point because not only is Dromm, to any sensible observer, a grotesque pervert and the antithesis of a role model, but he is also a congenital liar, and I'm referring specifically to that "ten percent" figure that he and all radical homosexuals lie about.

The ridiculous myth that homosexuals comprise ten percent of the population has been so thoroughly disproven and discredited for decades that only the truly naïve and uninformed grant it any currency. The homosexual movement knows this. For it is the uninformed that this particular lie is aimed at.

The origin of the ten percent myth is the 1948 report by Alfred Kinsey, "Sexual Behavior in the Human Male." Dr. Judith Reisman, in her book "Kinsey, Sex and Fraud: The Indoctrination of a People", probably documented the most thorough exposé of Kinsey's shoddy findings. In fact, the ten percent figure is so astoundingly false that it remains a wonder that people like Dromm actually think they can get away with it. Even the homosexual newspaper The Advocate refers to it as "that famous ten percent figure."

Focus on the Family has done a concise investigation on the history of the ten percent myth. They write, "This argument has been so overwhelmingly disproved… that it may be unnecessary to mention it. But on the chance that the reader may need to confront this claim in future discussions, we will briefly review what is commonly called the '10 percent myth' and how to respond to it. In 1948, sex researcher Alfred Kinsey published Sexual Behavior in the Human Male, which listed his findings after taking the sexual histories of 5,300 American men. The findings, especially on homosexuality, shocked American sensibilities: 37 percent of the subjects admitted at least one homosexual experience since their adolescence, and 10 percent claimed to have been homosexual for at least three years."

Focus on the Family continued, "Word was out — 10 percent of the male population was homosexual! Knowing there is power in numbers, pro-gay theorists and spokesmen repeated the statistic relentlessly until it became a given: one out of every 10 males was gay; therefore, homosexuality was much more common than anyone had previously thought. The concept was extremely useful to activists when, decades later, they would ask how anyone could believe ten percent of the population was abnormal, immoral or just plain wrong."

In addition, deliberately inflating the number of homosexuals makes politicians more likely to fear and acquiesce to them.

Focus on the Family went on, "First, Kinsey's data were not taken from a population accurately representing American men. Dr. Judith Reisman, in her book Kinsey, Sex and Fraud: The Indoctrination of a People has soundly discredited Kinsey's conclusions and methods. One of her important findings was that 25 percent of the men he surveyed were prisoners, many of whom were sex offenders. Naturally, [in the 1940's] a higher incidence of homosexuality would be found among prisoners, especially sex offenders, many of whom may have been in prison for homosexual behavior.

"Second, subsequent studies have disproved the 10 percent claim. USA Today reported on April 15, 1993, a new survey of 3,321 American men indicating 2.3 percent of them had engaged in homosexual behavior within the previous 10 years; only 1.1 percent reported being exclusively homosexual. This was only the latest in a series of studies proving Kinsey wrong. In 1989, a U.S. survey estimated no more than 6 percent of adults had any same-sex contacts and only 1 percent were exclusively homosexual; a similar survey in France found 4 percent of men and 3 percent of women had ever engaged in homosexual contacts, while only 1.4 percent of the men and 0.4 percent of the women had done so within the past five years. The article concluded, not surprisingly, that the 10 percent statistic proposed by Kinsey was 'dying under the weight of new studies.'"

And finally a statement of honesty from the movement. "A candid remark by a lesbian activist explains how the 10 percent figure stayed in the public's awareness for so long: 'The thing about the 'one in 10' – I think people probably always did know that it was inflated. But it was a nice number that you could point to, that you could say 'one in ten,' and it's a really good way to get people to visualize that we're here.' If what she's saying is true, gay spokesmen were willing to repeat something they knew to be false, for the sake of furthering their cause. [This] propaganda that people 'always knew was inflated,' [was] but promoted anyway because [in the minds of radical 'gays'] the end justified the means."

And speaking of Dromm being a "role model," in a letter to a school board member, he wrote, "Lesbians and gay men are about much more than sex. While we differ from heterosexuals in the choice of the object of our affection, we are also similar in many other ways. However, lesbians and gays also have a proud culture, history and role in our society. We have a rich, diverse culture of which we are very proud. We believe that it is about time for reasonable folks to sit down and to discuss this issue in a non-emotional, non-hysterical way."

First of all, what kind of culture emanates from a group that defines itself by its sexual perversions? Unlike a racial or ethnic culture, which is defined by blood, language or geographic location, homosexuality is defined by behavior. And the legacy of this culture is an average life expectancy for a homosexual male of about 40, due to the horrible spread of disease caused by a lifestyle of uncontrolled grotesque perversity.

According to Stanley Monteith, M.D., "The tragedy is that most people in the general population do not understand what the homosexual lifestyle really involves. The young people in our schools are being indoctrinated in their sex education classes with the idea that homosexuality is simply an alternative lifestyle… 100% of homosexuals engage in fellatio; 93% engage in rectal sex; 92% engage in something called 'rimming' (licking in and around your partner's anus); 29% in 'golden showers' (urinating on other men); 17% in 'scat' (rolling around in human feces.) In addition, male homosexuals average between 20 and 106 partners every year – averaging 300 to 500 in a lifetime. 37% engage in sadomasochism; 20% have engaged in sodomy with more than 1,000 men. Compared to heterosexuals, male homosexuals are eight times more likely to acquire hepatitis, 14 times more likely to have syphilis, and *5,000 times more likely to acquire AIDS.*" (Emphasis added.)

So with Dromm's colorful history as a backdrop, it might appear inconceivable that no elected official ever spoke out against him, especially since he became more and more of a public figure. It goes without saying, of course, that as his notoriety grew, no school board member ever spoke out against him either. The only support I received was from Howard Hurwitz, the columnist, retired public school principal, president of the Family Defense Council and author of the book, "The Last Angry Principal." Tracking my battle with Dromm closely, Hurwitz was relentless with his letters to government officials and the New York City schools chancellor, but only I had any real power. It took every maneuver I could think of to shame school board members into assisting me to stop Dromm. Ultimately, it didn't work.

As time went on, his principal Birbiglia retired, and Dromm evidently felt more unconstrained. He was constantly in the press and, incredibly, after being scolded and warned, Dromm committed the very same offense he had perpetrated four years earlier. In yet another letter to the editor, this time to the Queens Ledger, and once again in response to a column by Hurwitz, Dromm stated that he was "open about my homosexuality with my students."

When I read it, I nearly fell off my chair. In the letter, Dromm claimed to have the support of two parent association presidents and certain school board members. Then he wrote, "Perhaps they also understand that I serve as a positive role model to the children in my class, especially to the 10 percent who will eventually grow up to be gay or lesbian." There he goes again.

And finally, "...I play a highly visible role in the Queens lesbian liberation movement... and am open about my homosexuality with my students."

Unbelievably, Dromm brought the next wave of opposition upon himself because he couldn't control his own need to boast about violating district policy. The letter set several things in motion. Since I was virtually assured of getting no help from the other board members or other elected officials, I could enlist only Hurwitz to buttress my own efforts.

I immediately sent a memorandum to our superintendent, Joseph Quinn, who was responsible for handling disciplinary and personnel matters. I wrote, in part, "It is clear from the attached letter to the editor which appeared in last week's Queens Ledger, that the hysterical homosexual, Daniel P. Dromm, who teaches at PS 199, still cannot control his outrageous behavior. It is also quite clear that Mr. Dromm never actually obeyed the instructions from his supervisor, Principal Jack Birbiglia, who ordered him to refrain from discussing his perversions in any manner while in the presence of his fourth grade class... Being well-connected to school board members does not grant him special privilege to violate district policy and the reprimand he has already received for past activity. Please let me know how you intend to proceed with this matter."

Quinn responded two months later that the Office of Legal Services felt there was "nothing of substance." I was furious, and wrote a second memo. "It is inconceivable that the investigation of Mr. Daniel Dromm's activities led to 'nothing of substance...' This is a very curious manner in which to investigate – not questioning the very person involved in the inappropriate behavior. A further irony is that it was Mr. Dromm himself who provided the evidence which prompted the investigation in the first place."

I continued, "It is incomprehensible to me, to say the least, that a man publicly admits to doing something... does not deny it, brags about it in his homosexual newsletter, and is not questioned at all. What kind of investigation is this?"

Hurwitz wrote directly to the chancellor, reiterating these points, and added, "It is clear that Superintendent Quinn has no intention of bringing charges against Mr. Dromm. Therefore, we are requesting that you order Mr. Quinn to take the appropriate action. If he fails to do so promptly, we request that you supersede…"

Needless to say, Dromm went unscathed and unpunished. It was astounding how Dromm was being protected by the political powers in the school system.

Things began moving quickly as the incident sparked a new flurry of citywide news coverage. Strangely, Dromm began to backtrack somewhat, telling the media that he never actually initiated conversations about his homosexuality, but was merely responding to a question by a student. But his original letter said nothing of the sort and, in fact, was very general. It did not point to one specific instance in which a student questioned him. It strains credulity to the extreme that, based on his own previous words, Dromm had never initiated these conversations.

But he told the Queens Ledger, "Once in a blue, blue moon, a student will make a reference to me being gay. If I am directly asked, I will tell them; however, I have never initiated a conversation with any of my students about my homosexuality."

Not only is this statement belied by Dromm's own previous statements, but in a separate letter to the school board two years earlier, he attached a newspaper article which promoted the idea of discussing homosexuality openly with students. He wrote, "We are writing to call your attention to the enclosed article which proposes that adults discuss lesbian and gay love openly with children."

In the Ledger article, Hurwitz said, "If Quinn and Chancellor Crew do not act at once, they are unprincipled. If Quinn doesn't proceed promptly to remove Dromm, then he is beneath contempt."

It was somewhat curious that Dromm was backing off, considering he seemed to be winning all the political battles. It could be that officials were getting tired of protecting him and somewhat embarrassed, as I continued to expose his actions to the public.

The Ethical Culture Society of Queens sent a signed petition to the school board condemning me. "The committee discussed Mr. Borzellieri's mean-spirited attacks on Mr. Daniel Dromm and voted to express support for Mr. Dromm and condemnation for Mr.

Borzellieri's scurrilous smear tactics." The letter also said that I would have been well served to have observed their recent program honoring Martin Luther King.

First of all, who the hell ever heard of the Ethical Culture Society of Queens? And second, some groups simply have too much time on their hands.

As the controversy continued to roar, I was sent articles in the "gay" press in New York which, as one can imagine, is fairly influential with politicians. The newsletter of Q-GLU (Queens Gay and Lesbian United) wrote, "Homophobia has been around for sometime. Nowhere in Queens has it been more evident than in District 24. Distortion and ignorance are a bigot's chief weapons... so Frank Borzellieri and Howard Hurwitz, both columnists for the Queens Ledger Newspaper Group, press for disciplinary action against Mr. Dromm."

But disciplinary action against Dromm was going nowhere, so I decided to take a more pro-active role. Since Dromm was discussing his homosexuality with impunity with 10 year olds, I decided to pay his school a visit and observe his class. I left word with the principal that I would be at the school in the morning and would be observing several classes, with Dromm's being one of them.

While school board members do not, except under rare circumstances, get involved in personnel matters, it was not only the right but the obligation of school board members to visit schools and observe classes, whenever they can. Clearly, my purpose in going to PS 199 was to show Dromm that I was taking a special interest in his school because of his actions. It was not my intention to confront Dromm in his classroom, not only because that would be a disruption but because Dromm would never commit a violation with me there anyway.

Board members visit schools regularly without a ripple, but news that I was going to PS 199 spread like wildfire. Upon arriving at the school, I was greeted by the deputy superintendent August Saccoccio, who was in the principal's office. "Frank," he said immediately, "you're overstepping your authority." I replied, "Aren't you embarrassed covering for this guy? Besides, you have no authority over school board members. We have authority over you. Now I'm here to observe classes. You're welcome to join me. If you don't like it, you can leave."

I observed Dromm's class for a few minutes and knew my visit to the school would cause a stir. And sure enough, Dromm spread the word that I was out to get him. His own organization's newsletter described recent events in an article titled, "Homophobes Attack QLGPC Co-chair Again." After rehashing the Hurwitz article and the Dromm letter to the editor, the article stated, "Mostly, Dromm has chosen not to respond to Hurwitz' attacks, believing that most people think he is nuts anyway… He [Dromm] reiterated that firing a teacher on the basis of sexual orientation is illegal in New York City."

Another Dromm lie. We were not going after him for his sexual "orientation," but for discussing his perversions with young children.

The article continued, "Not to stop the homophobes. Less than a week after Dromm's letter to the editor was published 'the enforcer,' (anti-multicultural education, anti-Martin Luther King holiday, anti-gay) school board member and another Jackson Heights News columnist, Frank Borzellieri showed up at Dromm's school for a 'tour' with the Deputy Superintendent. Never had Borzellieri been there before. Hmmmm. One doesn't need to be a Rhodes scholar to know why Borzellieri had really come…. Dromm is expecting an increased level of attacks from these characters… While Dromm has not been fired from his job, the homophobes on the school board have sure made life miserable for him."

I agreed to give my first and only interview to the biggest and most influential "gay" newspaper in New York, the New York Blade. I had no interest in speaking with a paper that would undoubtedly be biased against me, and would not even be read by anyone I knew. But the reporter, Katie Szymanski, was pleasant and professional, so I told her I didn't care if they editorialized against me, I just wanted to be quoted accurately. And the article was surprisingly fair and, at times, even funny, even though she quoted no one who was on my side besides me.

The front page article titled, "Battle brews at P.S. 199:

Dismissal of gay teacher is a crusade for Queens School Board Member," led with the results of that so-called investigation that cleared Dromm of any wrongdoing and stated that it was the second time in five years I had demanded an investigation into his behavior. When asked about the non-support from the school board, I called them a "very irresponsible and cowardly lot." Chan was also interviewed about the banning of the four words.

Dromm stated, "If a married teacher said, 'I went upstate this weekend with my wife,' they never would have questioned his reference to his sexuality."

I responded, "He's assuming that's a moral equivalency. He thinks saying, 'I went away with my wife' is the same as saying 'I slept with my boyfriend.'"

The article noted the recent involvement of radical homosexual New York City Councilman Tom Duane, who, along with 27 other elected officials, sent a letter to the chancellor requesting that "measures be taken" against me to discourage my "ongoing campaign of harassment" against Dromm.

"Beyond the terrible hardship that it imposes upon Mr. Dromm," the letter said, "this campaign only serves to distract from his ability to focus his energy and talents on teaching and serving his students." Two local leftists signed the letter, Councilmen John Sabini and Walter McCaffrey; the other signatories were from other parts of the city.

McCaffrey, who is a lame intellect, said, "[The school board] has to recognize that while it represents some of the most conservative neighborhoods in America, that does not give them license to ignore reality." Who is this "them" McCaffrey speaks of? I was the only one trying to stop Dromm.

The article's author, commenting on my overall anti-multicultural view, wrote, "Borzellieri's opinions are considered so inflammatory that some people have questioned why he should be allowed to remain in a position where he can affect decisions about the education of public school students."

I'm "allowed" (as if I have someone's permission) to remain because of these annoying little details called election results. I was elected, re-elected, then re-elected again.

Even the left-wing United Federation of Teachers union half-heartedly agreed. "The [UFT] believes there would be no legal basis for removing Borzellieri, who was elected to his office."

A UFT official named Ron Davis was quoted, "His opinions don't constitute ethnic slurs. While unpopular, they don't rise to the level of criminality."

Well, that's a relief! And by the way, unpopular with whom?

The article noted that Dromm was angry that the union had not done more for him. Davis replied, "I think what Mr. Dromm was told is that nobody is taking any action against him, so there is nothing for us to defend. I wouldn't consider this harassment because Mr. Borzellieri has a reputation for shooting off his mouth, and only embarrasses himself when he does so."

In the end, the outrageous actions Dromm revealed in his letter to the editor would culminate with two new resolutions I put forth. Although they did not mention Dromm by name, everyone knew that they were targeted at him and anyone else who dared to be so brazen.

My resolutions were very specifically worded in order to close that silly loophole about discussing the four words outside the sex ed curriculum. I would also word them in order to put enormous pressure on the other board members. The white liberal hypocrites on the board, who came from the lily-white conservative parts of the district and pretended to their neighbors to be conservative, then voted like flaming leftists on the board, would have to stand up and be counted. The greater pressure would come from the radical homosexual lobby, and the cowardly board would vote with the "gays" at first, but eventually board members would be forced to reverse themselves.

With Garkowski also retired now, I would have to carry the argument by myself. The resolutions were similar, one focusing on conduct by teachers in the school and one more a statement on the values of the district. My first resolution stated, in part, "Resolved, that Community School Board 24 establish the following policy with regard to discussion *with students within the schools* of homosexuality, abortion, contraception and masturbation: *Forbid the discussion with students by all employees, *within the confines of school grounds and/or on school time*, of homosexuality, abortion, contraception and masturbation. *Discussion of these topics shall be forbidden during class, whether as part of instruction or an informal manner. *…forbidden… even if initiated by the student.

"This [policy] is in keeping with the spirit of this district's current policy deleting any references to the [four topics in its current sex ed curriculum]" and that "questions on sensitive issues be referred to the parents and that values representing the morality of our community be positively represented."

I did make the point independent of the resolution, because I anticipated some silly opposition, that "discussion" of abortion to older middle school students was not precluded when taught in history class regarding, say, Roe vs. Wade. Everyone knew "discussion" meant as an option or policy opinion.

My second resolution was more a statement that our policies should reflect the values of the community. It stated, in part, "Resolved that this School Board affirms its belief that to equate homosexuality (a lifestyle) with race, ethnicity and religion – either morally or socially – is contrary to the beliefs of our community, and be it further resolved that… to equate homosexuality or heterosexual marriage – either morally or socially – is contrary to the beliefs of our community."

These resolutions were absolute killers to board members. I don't think certain board members ever hated me more than they did this night because they were entirely boxed into a corner. The radical homosexuals, to whom they were in thrall, were placing enormous pressure on them, but their neighbors and the average people in the community would be horrified if they found out they had voted against these proposals – and board members knew I would certainly see to that.

Even one newspaper editor told me that in a private conversation a board member expressed to him that they were thinking of ways to try and avoid the vote altogether.

The roll call votes on both resolutions were as follows: For –

George Anastasiou, Frank Borzellieri, Mary Crowley; Against – Robert Cermeli, Louisa Chan, Sharon Geremia, Catherine Marlowe, Katherine Masi, Linda Sansivieri.

After the meeting, Dromm was jubilant, but board members on the winning side (excepting Chan) were furious and panic-stricken. Dromm was quoted in the press saying, "It's a major defeat for Frank Borzellieri." And indeed it was, but I wasn't finished yet. In addition to the press coverage revealing the way board members had voted, I continued to do talk shows, naming board members by name, and slamming them mercilessly for betraying the community. Board members took a beating, probably in a worse manner than I ever knew.

I finally announced that I would be placing another resolution on the agenda for the next board meeting. Political realities being what they are, board members who were dying to make up for their shameful vote, could not simply vote yes on the identical resolution, so I negotiated a change that simply included all sexual discussion (including heterosexual.) The change was meaningless to me because normal teachers were not discussing their sexuality. My resolution's aim was identical, but the meaningless change gave board members, they believed, political cover. All that mattered to me was winning.

The media buildup was as expected once the resolutions were placed on the agenda for the next board meeting.

An article in the New York Post was titled, "Furor over bid to gag teachers on sex lives."

It stated, "A [school board] is set to vote on whether to forbid school employees from discussing their sex lives – a measure one openly gay teacher says is aimed at him…. Fellow board member Louisa Chan agreed that the rule is aimed specifically at gagging Dromm and other homosexual teachers."

The 60's radical and PTA president of PS 199 Mary Lazaro said, "I think it's homophobia."

Once again, Dromm backtracked on his previous statements, claiming he only acknowledged his homosexuality if asked.

At the meeting itself, I was quiet, smiling like the cat who was about to eat the canary. City Comptroller Alan Hevesi showed up again, erroneously believing I was going to lose. He was prepared to gloat, but was instead humiliated when the vote went in my favor. Clearly, he came to the meeting completely uninformed, talking nonsense during the discussion phase. No board member responded to his drivel and the vote was taken. The roll call vote was eight to one in support, with only Chan having the courage to vote her true beliefs.

Parent leader Gloria Morgenstern told Newsday, "Basically, the parents supported the resolution. This is a very conservative district."

Dromm was understandably broken, but he should have been angry at the liberals who abandoned him. Nevertheless, within a short time, I received a letter from the Board of Education's Office of Equal Opportunity. It read, "The Office of Equal Opportunity is in receipt of a complaint of alleged sexual orientation discrimination from Mr. Daniel Dromm, in which you are the respondent.

"He claims you are intimidating him by visiting his classroom. No determination has been made concerning the validity of Mr. Dromm's complaint.

"In order to resolve this matter, please contact my office to schedule an interview…"

The complaint officer actually came to my apartment, briefcase in hand, and told me what had been alleged against me. I was fully prepared, with press clippings, Dromm's statements, letters to the editor, and an explanation of the role of the school board in all this. In other words, my actions were more than appropriate and warranted.

At the conclusion of the meeting, the officer patted me on the back as he left and said, in a deadpan and off the record manner, "Good luck to you." Within a week or so, he called me to tell me the case was thrown out.

Homosexual Candidate for Board 24

Having endured a string of defeats, and realizing they could not count on the cowardly liberals on Board 24, the homosexual movement attempted to snatch victory in the one area that they had not yet tried – run one of their own for the District 24 School Board. Imagine the retribution they would feel with that – winning a seat on the most notorious school board in the country, the very board that had defeated them over and over.

The candidate would be Wayne Mahlke, a sidekick of Dromm's who was also a frequent agitator at school board meetings. Mahlke was a true blue (lavender?) member of the radical movement and there was no denying that it would be a coup for a "gay" to land on this school board. This would be for the 1999 elections, my third and final term.

While Mahlke's campaign literature spoke of class size and reading skills, everyone knew Mahlke cared about those things about as much as Rosie O'Donnell cares about good manners. There was no doubt as to why Mahlke was really running – to promote the radical homosexual agenda. A fundraising letter signed by Dromm stated, "Just look at the endorsements he's stacked up only a couple of weeks into the campaign. That's because all those elected officials who have endorsed Wayne know he's good for children. After all, that's what this race is really all about. Wayne knows that teaching multiculturalism and acceptance for diversity is what will prepare our kids to become the next generation of New Yorkers.

"Wayne needs us to help him bring new ideas, new energy and an even temperament and focus to District 24, which has been plagued with craziness ever since the madness over the Children of the Rainbow curriculum... Let's get together and send a message to the powers that be that progressives like us do intend to change the status quo especially as it relates to District 24."

And of course, the letter would not have been complete without the use of my name to raise money. "Wayne has done all the leg work, pounded the streets, made all the contacts and is ready for the challenge. And what a challenge it will be. You can be sure bigots like School Board Member Frank Borzellieri will pull out all the stops as election day approaches."

Pull out all the stops was exactly what I had intended to do. But there were several problems. First of all, Mahlke and I had vastly different constituencies. Neither of us could ever get votes from the other's base of support. The white liberals on the board always pretended to be conservative when they campaigned, but I could more easily target them for defeat because they were appealing to the same white middle class voters as I was. Moreover, I always had the luxury of being able to tailor my campaign to target others for defeat because I was the only candidate who was assured of winning. I had done this successfully before, especially when I went right to Catherine Marlowe's stronghold – to her neighbors and to the surrounding community where she had been a popular principal. When I exposed her record, she was defeated.

In addition, Mahlke did indeed have a well-run campaign. He seemed to have volunteers everywhere, had impressive literature, and presented himself fairly well at candidate forums. And it was obvious he had raised a considerable amount of money. He was also smart enough to not mention the radical homosexual agenda when in public and especially when there was press around.

But I began, I believed, to figure out the strategy he would need to actually win. First of all, the number of voters who were truly committed to the "gay" agenda was relatively small. Even other radical non-white and multicultural groups didn't give a rat's ass about the homosexuals. So Mahlke would have his small base of support and would have to try and snooker other voting blocks.

And that is exactly what he was doing. He tried to run as a moderate in the conservative areas, so I exposed him. Naturally, Mahlke's candidacy attracted a lot of press attention, and I was always there as his antagonist. He refused to debate me one on one, but local television stations did features on the race, using both of us as opposite poles. It was Steve Dunleavy of the New York Post who at my urging wrote a column on the race, and who threatened to knock Mahlke's teeth out if he tried to impose the "rainbow" curriculum on his kids. Suddenly, none of the liberals were complaining about *this* "childless bachelor" running for the school board.

In a humorous incident, Mahlke's campaign created a piece using an endorsement by Al Sharpton and a photo of the two of them together, which was distributed only in the small black section of the district, which was a couple of housing projects. But I got hold of it, gave it to the local papers, and it was published for all the white middle class voters to see.

Still, the conventional wisdom seemed to be that Mahlke would manage to win. Some people even suggested that it would be good for me if he won, in that he would be the perfect foil for me to beat up on. But I rejected that as nonsense. There was no way I wanted to give the radical homosexual lobby any validation in my district. At one campaign stop, I asked Mahlke how things were looking for him. He replied, "Let's just say, Frank, that I expect to be up there with you when the new board meets." I responded jokingly that he had just admitted that I would win.

In the end, as the final votes were being tallied at the Board of Elections, with most of the candidates present, it was obvious that Mahlke would lose. He finished eleventh overall. I actually felt sorry for him at that moment because it's never easy for a candidate to lose an election. I told him that he had worked hard and did his best, which is all anyone can do. The truth is, with my own re-election assured, my sense about Mahlke's defeat was more one of relief than joy.

Recruitment

While Joseph Fernandez would undoubtedly have the reputation as the most pro-homosexual education chancellor in New York City history because of his advocacy of the "rainbow" curriculum, the fact is that Harold Levy's record of support for the radical homosexual movement was easily the most sordid and horrific.

Harold Levy was an appointed political hack who got the job because the unelected central Board of Education, by a majority vote of four to three, handed him the job. Because he was so manifestly unqualified for the position, he needed a special waiver from the New York State legislature in order to take the position. The deciding vote that handed Levy the position was from his crony Terri Thomson, the appointed Queens County member of the central board, who was an underling of Levy's at their place of employment.

Ignoring an obvious conflict of interest, Thomson nonetheless voted for Levy and he assumed the job.

In the job, which he treated as a political fiefdom rather than an educational position, Levy's grotesque affinity for "gay" causes was so stark that he essentially functioned as an advance man for homosexual sodomy.

The first paragraph of an article in the New York Post said it all. "Attention gay and lesbian teachers: Schools Chancellor Harold Levy wants you as new classroom recruits." Thanks to Levy, the Board of Education became the first New York City agency to ever overtly recruit homosexuals. The "Gay Life Expo" at the Jacob Javits Center in Manhattan was the venue for Levy's repulsive social activism.

I was quoted in the article stating, "It is typical of the immoral agenda of the left-wing powers that control the Board of Education under the misleadership of Harold Levy that they would celebrate perversion and seek to recruit sodomites… Who will they recruit next, necrophiliacs and those into bestiality?"

Dromm, of course, was quoted, "It's a good thing. It's a move in the right direction." The article added, "He [Dromm] urged Levy to remove Borzellieri from the school board for violating the school system's anti-discrimination policy by spouting 'vile and bigoted comments.'"

Sure, when you can't defeat a popularly elected board member at the ballot box, urge an unelected hack to remove him through dictatorial fiat. And I have one other question: how exactly does an agency actually "recruit" homosexuals to be teachers? I mean, what are they offered as incentive?

Boy Scouts

In a landmark decision on June 28, 2000, the United States Supreme Court ruled that the Boy Scouts of America had the right to exclude homosexuals as scout masters. The court's reasoning was based on upholding the right of a private organization to private association. In the case of the Scouts, it was their right to adhere to their own moral code. By the First Amendment, the court found, free people and free groups have the right to associate freely, and not have memberships or associations forced on them. Liberals usually worship at the altar of the Supreme Court, but, it turns out, only when the court rules in their favor. Principles have no place; it's only the results that matter.

Supreme Court ruling or not, the New York City Board of Education was having none of it. Once again, Harold Levy was at the forefront, sticking it to the Court and breaking all official ties with the Boy Scouts. Levy specifically revoked the Scouts opportunity to bid on future public school contracts and sponsorships. Now, in an overwhelmingly liberal city like New York, it was not surprising that individual school boards were passing their own resolutions both to condemn the Scouts and to deny them use of public school facilities. Even Mayor Rudy Giuliani had filed a court brief opposing the Boy Scouts.

For example, School Board 2 in Manhattan passed a resolution "withdrawing all sponsorship of and special privileges for the Boy Scouts of America (BSA) in response to the BSA's anti-gay membership policies." Board 2 President Karen Feuer wrote in a letter that Board 2 "is urging each of the other 31 Community School Boards to adopt a similar policy." She also urged districts to sever ties with a Scout-program called Learning for Life, which was in place in some city schools.

Naturally, I had other ideas. And once again, the other board members dreaded a repeat of the previous buildup and fallout caused by my previous resolutions. Within two months of the Board 2 actions gaining momentum, I put forth the only pro-Boy Scout resolution in the entire city.

It read, in part, "Whereas, the Boy Scouts of America have for 90 years functioned as a bedrock of moral values and principles and have been, and continue to be, a positive experience for millions of young men… and Whereas community School Board 24 supports the expressed policies and values of the Boy Scouts and rejects all attempts to undermine the Boy Scouts of America and its policies… Be it Resolved that Community School Board 24 supports continued sponsorship of Boy Scouts of America activities in District 24."

It was known before the meeting that I had the votes and the resolution would pass. When Board 24's support and my pending resolution became national news, the Boy Scouts of America were contacted for comment. Naturally, you would think the Scouts, under such fierce attack, would embrace the support of a major school board. Think again. In thrall to political correctness, the official Scout response was consistently pathetic and embarrassing. The Queens Tribune reported, "The Boy Scouts, in a released statement, were grateful for SB 24's stand and effort, but insist that they do not want the board to choose sides in an issue that will only result in further division."

That reminded me of the old joke about how a liberal is someone who can't take his own side in an argument. Not anymore. Official Boy Scouts rewrote the joke as anyone *attacked* by liberals can't take his own side.

The Scout presence at the school board meeting was just as disheartening. While the other side was out in full force, only one Scout advocate even spoke at all, and only about the practical effects of not permitting the Scouts to use school facilities, not about the moral issue at all. The contrast was embarrassing.

Wayne Mahlke was there and said, "Bigotry and intolerance is not acceptable in schools. What you're saying to the rest of the world is that in District 24, we welcome bigotry and intolerance!"

Daniel Dromm said, "Hatred is a lesson no child should ever learn."

Jimmy Van Bramer, a homosexual candidate for the city council, blasted the Scouts and said, "The organization I was once proud to be a part of would now exclude me because I am a gay man."

Outside of my own remarks, not one person on the board or in the audience, or of course the Scouts spokesmen themselves, defended the Scouts' right to ban homosexual scout masters or defended the basic moral argument.

Scout leader Walter Sanchez showed up with two other Scout leaders in jackets and ties, but he was the only one who even spoke.

He said, "We are not about sexuality, we are about first aid, leadership training, wilderness survival skills and building strong moral fiber for the children in our organization."

Sanchez continued, "Boy Scouts is about inclusion. Excluding us from recruiting in schools means that young boys will not be taught skills for living. The children who will suffer are the children who really need us. Those are the children from single parent families who need a male role model to teach them life skills."

Marie Vella, a Cub Scout mother, said, "We take trips to explore our neighborhood and we look to build character. That's what we are about."

Now, all of these comments are true enough, but ultimately beside the point. Sanchez and Vella clearly were purposely avoiding defending the Scouts on the moral issue. They were basically saying Scouts are good for boys, so ignore the moral issue even if you disagree with the Scouts' official position.

The few comments from board members were all in a similar vein. I asked board member Robert Cermeli before the meeting if he would defend the Scouts. He told me no, that he would only defend their right to use the school buildings and facilities. At the meeting, he said, "We shouldn't put the children in the middle of ideological battles of adults. For that reason I support the organization and the resolution." Only Chan voted against.

I expect this kind of cowardly nonsense from the board, but from the Scouts I couldn't believe it. After all that was done to come to their defense, and after I refused to soften the language in my resolution, they were more concerned about being politically correct than doing the right thing.

Because victory was certain and that was all that mattered, I simply let the vote take place after I had my say. I publicly defended the Scouts' policy but did not criticize the Scouts for refusing to defend themselves. But privately, I thought the Boy Scouts' reaction both nationally and locally was disgraceful. And I privately told Sanchez just that.

In an opinion column in the Daily News I wrote, "What has America come to when one of the nation's last vestiges of bedrock moral values can be trampled upon in clear defiance of the American tradition?"

Human Events supported my efforts and wrote, "In line with the ever more radical inversion of good and evil pursued by the left, New York City Schools Chancellor Harold Levy has decided to eliminate any official school connection with, or assistance to, local Boy Scouts of America troops. He used the scouts' affirmation of the traditional moral code regarding homosexuality as justification." Human Events then quoted from my op-ed piece in the Daily News.

When the news hit that the resolution had passed, conservatives and religious organizations were joyful. I received many calls and letters of thanks from parents of Scouts, but nothing from any local or national official Boy Scouts of America person or group.

Victory on Election Day

My detractors were always somewhat confounded by my "happy warrior" demeanor. Of course, I wasn't happy about the disastrous educational performance of the district and I was quite unhappy indeed about the gross infestation of multicultural materials in our schools. And I was certainly not happy that I lost virtually every vote that mattered (especially knowing *in advance* that I would lose.) Still, especially during my first term when most of the controversies were taking place, my detractors – and I'm speaking specifically about board members, audience members and politicians who regularly hurled their invective at me – were both confused and frustrated that their attacks never deterred me or prevented me from coming back the very next month with more of my ammunition. After they believed (erroneously) that they had beaten me down and that I would be subdued, they became frustrated when I would invite – some would say relish – the chance to go at it again, and the sooner the better.

There were several reasons why I gained strength and fire after these monthly soirées. First, it was simply a personality thing – I enjoy the fight and the rough and tumble of going at it on issues. But that aside, there were more practical reasons. I especially reveled in beating my detractors' brains in on intellectual matters. Even though they outnumbered me, their arguments amounted to little more than name-calling and liberal clichés. They never presented a true, rational, reasoned defense of their left-wing positions. Moreover, I never lost sight of the fact that everything I was doing and enduring at school board meetings was for public consumption. I knew I was reaching the normal citizens of New York because press coverage of our school board meetings was saturated. So although inside the four walls of the actual meeting I appeared to be "losing," I knew – always knew – that I was winning when it came to true public opinion. I would treat television talk shows the same way. On the Ricki Lake show, for example, the audience was typically hostile, but I knew I was really speaking to millions in

America and always received positive mail from regular New Yorkers and Americans after my appearances.

So not only was I reaching the true public with my actions at school board meetings, I was gaining its support. Moreover, I knew that all of this would bear fruit on election day.

The first time I ran for the school board I was virtually unknown to the public. There were a total of 24 candidates running to fill the nine seats and I personally knew only one of the other candidates. So school board members, candidates, and District 24 insiders had no idea who I was. (I was 30, and one candidate later joked that when she had read about my campaign platform, she pictured a 65 year old man.) The campaign came on the heels of the "rainbow" curriculum controversy, so turnout would be especially high. For the first time ever, all of New York City was aware of the school board elections.

All of my campaigns are alike and this first one was no different. I always run on three issues: anti-multicultural education, anti-bilingualism (favoring official English), and anti-"rainbow" (opposing the homosexual encroachment.) To a lesser extent, I focused on wasteful education spending and poor reading programs.

There was really no doubt in my mind that I would win, but I got the impression that other candidates weren't thinking about me much at all. When the smoke cleared and the results were tallied, Cummins, an 18-year veteran finished first, amidst her widespread publicity over "rainbow"; Garkowski, a Catholic priest and another 18-year vet, finished second, with the perennial backing of the district's parishioners. I came in a strong third, which was considered highly impressive in a field of 24 candidates.

District 24 insiders had two strong reactions to my victory, both hostile. First, there was a lot of resentment that this unknown newcomer had intruded on their little fiefdom of power. And second, when they found out what I stood for, the hostility was more like hatred. Now, in fairness, I was not treated this way by everyone, and with some people it was never personal. But overall, I knew I was unwelcome by virtually everyone on the inside. But I was elected and there wasn't anything they could do about it. My "fitness" for the board was questioned constantly during my first term. "He has

Victory on Election Day 167

no children in the schools! He's promoting an agenda!" I always answered the same way. I'm elected by the voters, including parents of the district's children, and every citizen's tax dollars are used to pay for the public schools. If you don't like it, defeat me at the next election. This standard response always annoyed them to no end.

Now fast forward three years to the next election campaign in 1996. Most of my public controversies and enormous incidents of sustained publicity occurred during my first three-year term. I was now the most famous school board member in the country. I was more well-known in New York City than most congressmen and others who held higher offices than I.

CANDIDATE'S NAME	Frank M. Borzellieri	培雷兆·布加果里
PUBLIC OFFICE	SCHOOL BOARD	DISTRICT 24

This is how Frank Borzellieri's name looked on the election ballot with his name translated into Chinese.

This next election presented a few problems for the left-wingers who had time and again vowed to defeat me. First, there was no chance of me losing. And second, they knew it. But worse than that, *I would be the one going after them.* Ain't we got fun!

The certainty that I would win, and win easily, was accepted, albeit unhappily, by the liberals. It was extremely painful for them not only for the obvious reason (they simply wanted me off the board), but because it was an acknowledgment that the public in reality agreed with my views. Now, of course, I always knew that the liberals secretly knew that their neighbors – the conservative white middle class voters of District 24 – agreed with me on the issues for which I was most famous, the racial and cultural issues that I railed about constantly. But to watch the candidates acquiesce to this reality during the campaign was pathetic and embarrassing for them (not to mention wildly unprincipled and cowardly.) I mean, here were people who had attacked me in the most vile and vicious manner imaginable, who had sworn a blood hatred of me, and who had essentially compared me with Satan, all within the secure and friendly confines of monthly school board meetings. Here now was their big chance – to attack me in the same manner that they had promised to, but now in front of the whole community at various campaign appearances, in front of the normal ordinary citizens of District 24 comprising the audiences. Fat chance.

People who attended Catholic primary schools in the old days will appreciate this analogy. The old nuns wore black and white from head to toe and inspired nothing less than terror in us students. They were mean for no reason, growled at us when they were in a good mood, and smacked us around constantly, usually for a grievous offense like making too much noise when dotting our i's. We all remember when Sister would bang our heads against the blackboard or smack our hands with a metal ruler. If you had a lay teacher, things were fine. But if you had one of those nuns, watch out.

But a funny thing would happen on two types of occasions – when parents would come to observe the class, or when a priest would visit. Suddenly, Sister would become Glenda, the kind witch of the North from the Wizard of Oz. Sister would smile, joke, laugh, and do her best impression of Mr. Rogers. We kids would all look at each other with these incredulous expressions on our faces, as if to say, "Who is this person?"

Well, all of that came back to me when I was observing all those liberal school board members campaigning outside the friendly four walls of school board meetings and in front of people who were my natural supporters. Not only did they never speak a solitary word against me, they would often preface their remarks with expressions like, "As Mr. Borzellieri says…" or "You may be aware that Mr. Borzellieri advocates…" They implied identification with me and suggested that somehow we were pals!

But I was a little more savvy than I had been in third grade and I wouldn't let them get away with it. One particular instance, while typical, stands out. It was a candidates' night at the Glendale Taxpayers Association. I got up first to make my remarks and began a diatribe against bilingual education. "Students should be taught in English only. That's how it was done for my parents. Nobody catered to our ancestors. If you came to America you were expected to learn and speak English." (Clapping and approving nods from the audience.) "Bilingual education is advocated by radical cultural aliens who have no desire to force people to assimilate to the United States and by those who have no loyalty to America." (Louder clapping and approving shouts of support.) "Those who push bilingual education on us, and use your tax dollars to do so, are groups like La Raza, a radical Hispanic group that wants Mexico to take over the southwest United States." (Concerned and outraged looks on the faces in the audience.) "Liberals in Albany and Washington who have sold you out in order to pander to these radicals are big advocates of bilingual education, even though they know it's a failure. But kissing up to these radicals is more important to them than defending traditional American culture and protecting your money." (Defiant and angry nods of the head, as if to express displeasure.) "As you know, I have been out there fighting against this alien monstrosity called bilingual education and I will continue to do so as long as I'm on that school board." (Raucous shouts and applause.) "Oh, and by the way, there is one more group who totally supports bilingual education 100 percent of the time: the rest of the school board including those who are here tonight as candidates!" (Angry glares at the other candidates, with stunned-type looks, as if to say, "What?!")

As you can imagine, there were probably wet piles underneath the chairs of every school board member in that room. As you can also guess, not one of those cowards dared to take me on, or even attempted to defend their monolithic votes in favor of bilingualism as they had so smugly done at all those school board meetings. Needless to say, these candidate forums did not do them much good and, in fact, caused them considerable embarrassment.

(Hey, I'm actually appreciative of most of the nuns from the old days, who taught us to read and write, and many of whom were down to earth.)

School board elections were no different than any other election in that every registered voter was eligible, and members were elected by the true voting public of the entire district. The only difference was that they were held in May instead of November, so turnout was always lower, in much the same way that turnout is lower for September primaries. Campaigns were also run in the conventional way, consisting of targeted mailings, flyers, phone banks, and as many campaign appearances as you could possibly make. District 24 campaigns, probably more than any other in New York, also benefited from considerable media coverage. Although New York City's school board voting system is a little complicated, in the end the top nine vote getters are elected. The press weighed in with advance coverage, reporting on candidate forums and appearances, as well as candidates' answers to questionnaires.

So running for re-election the first time in 1996, and because I was not only certain to win, but expected to finish first overall, I had the luxury of using my vote-getting ability to knock one of the liberals out. I targeted Catherine Marlowe because her base of support was not only smaller than some of the other candidates who were well-connected with the Queens Democratic Party machine, but also because the people who liked her also liked me.

Marlowe was popular with basically two groups of people. The first was the residents of the surrounding area of a school in Maspeth where Marlowe had been principal before she retired. The technical names for these areas of residents in New York are "election districts" or "e.d.'s" for short. They are simply geographic areas consisting of streets of registered voters. Candidates are free to check past voting trends to see where a particular candidate's strength is. For example, a candidate usually wins his home election district for obvious reasons – it consists of the immediate surrounding blocks in which he lives. But you can check all election districts in order to find out exactly where a candidate's votes came from in past elections. That's what I did with Marlowe. And indeed her voters came largely from these election districts surrounding her old school, PS 153 in Maspeth. She was also popular with a group of parents whose children were in a gifted and talented program that began in PS 153 when she was principal. I was enormously popular with that group because that gifted and talented program was the only program I ever supported, and also because they were white middle class conservative people.

How Marlowe could possibly be popular with either of these groups is because she was principal there, but also because she hid her extreme liberal voting record from them. Alas, I would put an end to that. The key thing was for me to assume people in those election districts liked us both, but to convince them to vote for me first. All I had to do was pound away on the issues and take enough votes away from Marlowe to cause her to finish tenth or lower.

Marlowe was one of the favorites to win because she was an incumbent and had been around for a long time. She was a low-key board member with a down-the-line liberal voting record. She rarely spoke up at board meetings. In fact, I only had one public confrontation with her. Her pet program was some silly self-esteem nonsense called "Reaching Out" that she placed on the agenda once a year for board approval. The wording of her resolution had a line about respecting cultures "equally." I asked her, "How many cultures?" She responded, "All cultures." I countered, "Are you saying all cultures are equally deserving of respect?" She answered, "What is your point?"

I then spelled it out for her. "Are you saying that we should respect cultures that practice female genital mutilation?"

When she finally caught on, she responded, "Mr. Borzellieri is baiting us."

I said, "You have an obligation to answer questions about your resolution, especially if you expect us to vote for it. Will you change your wording to indicate that American culture is superior to other cultures?"

Naturally, she wouldn't, and just as naturally the resolution passed.

When the Queens Ledger called me for an interview for an article they were doing on the campaign, I told the publisher, Walter Sanchez (who is also the Boy Scout leader from the previous chapter), that I was targeting Marlowe for defeat and I told him how. When the Ledger wrote its predictions for the school board election and picked me to finish first, the paper wrote, "His conservative philosophy on which he does not compromise, has brought him unparalleled attention. Love him or hate him, he has the courage of his convictions and represents the views of his constituents... his voters would probably go through a tornado to vote for him." The Ledger picked Marlowe to win by finishing fourth, but added, "If there is to be a shocking loss in this election, however, it could be Marlowe."

Sanchez, whose newspaper took full credit for this brilliant prediction, without disclosing that I had tipped him off that I was targeting Marlowe, made up for the slight by hiring me as a columnist two years later. When the avalanche of my votes fell on election day, it was indeed lights out for Marlowe.

By any standard, even the most cynical and hateful of me, the election totals were an astounding vindication for me, after all I had been made to endure. I not only finished with the most votes, but I totaled *three times as many votes as the second-place finisher*.

Press coverage gave conservatives their due. Newsday's headline was (pun intended, I believe), "Right Man For Queens School Post: Activist basks in victory." It began, "He battles sex education, bilingual classes and 'multicultural' books such as 'Young Martin's Promise' by the late, noted author Alex Haley.

"But it hasn't hurt conservative school board member Frank Borzellieri in the borough of Queens... its tope vote-getter. 'My critics said for three years that I was wrong,' said Borzellieri. 'Well, now I've proven them wrong by a mile.'

"Borzellieri, who grew up in the district and attended Catholic schools, has a reputation as a bullhorn on social issues."

The Daily News article, "Incumbent tops in ed race," stated, "Conservative incumbent Frank Borzellieri topped the list of nine winners... [he] claimed his first-place finish was a 'victory of stunning proportions. My win is a vindication of all that I stood for.'"

The Queens Ledger wrote, "So massive was the scope of the Borzellieri juggernaut, amassing triple the votes of the second-place finisher... Borzellieri achieved his victory by running on the very same issues that caused so much controversy during his first term." I was quoted, "Clearly, this proves I was right all along. The jackals who spent the last three years demanding my resignation should have a long talk with some of their neighbors. The people in this community do not want bilingual or multicultural education."

The article also pointed out that I won the neighborhoods of Ridgewood, Glendale, Maspeth, Middle Village and Elmhurst, and even pulled in votes from immigrant areas where I was thought to have little support, but where pockets of conservative whites still came out for me.

The Queens Gazette wrote, "Frank Borzellieri, the young, outspoken conservative board member from Ridgewood [had] an impressive vote tally…[he] has taken extremely conservative positions on the board against multi-culturalism and in favor of using English-only as the only language to be used in the schools. This was strongly opposed by the other board members…"

The Queens Tribune called the results, "A sharp conservative turn in District 24… Borzellieri, the fiery conservative who has received national attention for his previous stands against multiculturalism… was the clear-cut frontrunner… [his] victory was three times the size of the second-place finisher."

Afterword

School boards were dissolved by the New York State legislature in 2004, although I had no intention of running again. They were replaced by unelected, appointed committees of some sort with no power whatsoever. I was elected for three terms, from 1993 to 2004. In the short time since the boards were eliminated, nothing has changed educationally. My complaints, however, are two-fold. First, I have the same complaint that I always had – the abominable condition of the public school system in the country and particularly in New York City, due to failed anti-American left-wing approaches.

But my bigger complaint was the impetus for this book. As I made clear in the introduction, this was not a book about the disastrous condition of public education per se, although that obviously occupied virtually all the pages. Rather, it was about the treatment of a conservative on a New York City school board who actually tries to buck the system by turning sacred liberal cows into hamburger and challenging liberal orthodoxies like a true heretic.

Regarding this second complaint, I fear that things are as bad as ever. If school boards were brought back into existence in New York City today, and I were to change my name and go incognito and get myself elected all over again, I would have to endure the same brutal treatment I went through in my first eleven years.

The point is that the bestial attacks on anyone who dares to speak a different point of view continue today. Conservatives are physically threatened, shouted down, require security and have their speaking engagements cancelled at many universities.

Anyone who dares impart those "secret" unspoken truths about race and culture risks his career. And forget about any "conservative" Republican official support. Only the free-thinking conservative ideological movement was there supporting my efforts, as were the average voters and citizens. Unfortunately, those who control the true reins of power are more concerned with political correctness and sucking up to the thought police. To hell with our

Eurocentric American culture and the state of education.

Until a discernibly large number of people are not afraid to speak out on these ultra-sensitive issues, I fear the brutal unforgiving censors will continue to stifle dissent. More times than I can count I've been approached by people over the years who tell me, "You say out loud what people think privately or say in the privacy of their living rooms."

What does this say about free speech and discourse in America? By documenting the treatment I received, it is my hope to call attention to this travesty, and to galvanize conservatives and all decent patriotic Americans to defend their country and their culture.

Rogues Gallery of Liberals

Louisa Chan
School Board Member
100% Liberal Voting Record
Native of China. Devout liberal was often the leader of the opposition and on the vanguard of extreme liberal causes.

Elizabeth Gambino
School Board Member
100% Liberal Voting Record
White liberal fanatic who conspired with other leftists on the board to block pro-American books from entering the schools and libraries.

Jake LaSala
School Board Member
100% Liberal Voting Record
White liberal hypocrite who claims to love multiculturalism but shields himself and his family from non-whites by living in a safe, lily-white neighborhood.

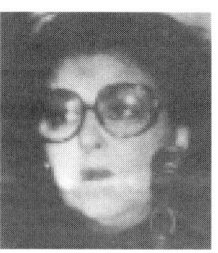

Linda Sansivieri
School Board Member
99% Liberal Voting Record
Another white liberal hypocrite who claims to love multiculturalism and integration but lives apart from non-whites in a safe, lily-white neighborhood.

Kathy Masi
School Board Member
99% Liberal Voting Record
Another white liberal hypocrite who claims to love multiculturalism and integration but lives apart from non-whites in a safe, lily-white neighborhood.

Catherine Marlowe
School Board Member
99% Liberal Voting Record
Another white liberal hypocrite who claims to love multiculturalism and integration but lives apart from non-whites in a safe, lily-white neighborhood.

Rogues Gallery of Liberals

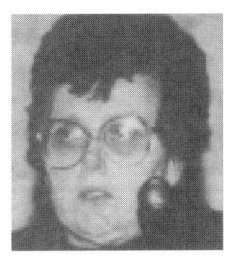

Mary Crowley
School Board Member
98% Liberal Voting Record

White liberal who supported all multicultural and bilingual programs, squandering tens of millions of dollars on anti-Americanism.

Rev. John Garkowski
School Board Member
80% Liberal Voting Record

Catholic priest who supported all multicultural and bilingual programs, but opposed the homosexual influence on the board.

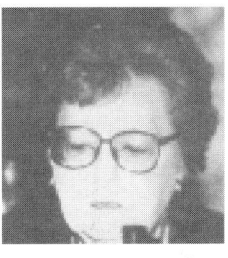

Mary Cummins
School Board Member
66% Liberal Voting Record

Despite opposing homosexual influence on the board, supported wasting tax dollars on multiculturalism and opposed American cultural superiority.

Robert Cermeli
School Board Member
99% Liberal Voting Record

White liberal who voted for all multicultural and bilingual programs, squandering millions of tax dollars on anti-American nonsense.

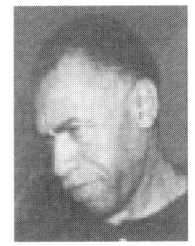

Perry Buckley
School Board Member
100% Liberal Voting Record

First black elected to Board 24. Arrested for murdering his white mistress. Fanatical supporter of all left-wing causes.

Daniel Dromm
Teacher in District 24

Radical homosexual who "outed" himself in front of his fourth grade class and who had been previously arrested for engaging in homosexual sex in a parking lot.

Lynched

Rogues Gallery of Liberals

Wayne Mahlke
Candidate for School Board 24
Radical homosexual who ran a losing campaign for the school board on a platform of increasing grotesque homosexual and multicultural programs in the schools.

Ramon Cortines
New York City Schools Chancellor
Publicly opposed all efforts to add pro-American books to the schools and to acknowledge the superiority of Western culture in the curriculum.

Harold Levy
New York City Schools Chancellor
Ultraliberal who banned the Boy Scouts from conducting regular business in the schools and who promoted the recruitment of homosexual teachers.

Alan Hevesi
New York City Comptroller
As New York State Comptroller was arrested and forced out of office for defrauding the state government. Another white liberal hypocrite who says he loves integration but lives in a safe lily-white neighborhood.

The Only Conservative

100% Conservative Voting Record
Frank Borzellieri, upon his election to the school board in 1993.

Print Media Sources

Surabhi Avasthi, "Book fight lost, sez backer," *Daily News*. February 9, 1995.
M. Paul Jackson, "School Book proposal Blocked At SB 24 Meeting," *Queens Ledger*. February 16, 1995.
"Schools win OK to pick own books," *Daily News*. February 15, 1995.
John Toscano, "Multiculturalism Debate Reignited; Call For More Pro-America Books," *Queens Gazette*. January 19, 1995.
John Toscano, "Board 24 Refutes Borzellieri's Bid To Ban Anti American Books," *Queens Gazette*. February 2, 1995.
John Toscano, "Chancellor Chides Borzellieri For Denigration Of Other Cultures," *Queens Gazette*. February 16, 1995.
Robert Trotta, "New Committee To Decide Fate Of Book Resolution At School Board 24," *Times Newsweekly*. February 16, 1995.
"What's the Resolution?" *Queens Ledger*. February 2, 1995.
Jeff Simmons, "Schools' book flap rages on in Queens," *New York Post*. February 1, 1995.
Linda Ocasio, "Candidate pushes new history view," *Daily News*. February 1, 1995.
Linda Ocasio, "Book foe turns over a new leaf," *Daily News*. January 25, 1995.
Rose Kim, "Queens Pol Pushes His Reading List," *Newsday*. October 11, 1994.
Editorial, *Times Newsweekly*. June 23, 1994.
Rose Kim, "Jeers for Multiculturalism Foe," *Newsday*. June 24, 1994.
Leonard Klie, "CSB 24 Rejects Borzellieri's Stance on Multicultural Ed," *Times Newsweekly*. June 23, 1994.
John Toscano, "Borzellieri Loses Schl. Bd 24 Skirmish," *Queens Gazette*. June 30, 1994.
"Cultural Superiority in Curriculum Rejected," *New York Times*. June 24, 1994.
Marcia Gelbart, "Board Member: American Culture Is Best," *Queens Tribune*. June 30, 1994.
"Ignorance Is Dangerous," *District 24 Update*. September/October 1994.
"New York City district says No to controversial "America First' policy," *The American School Board Journal*. August 1994.
Patricia Mangan, "No 'superiority' lessons," *Daily News*. June 22, 1994.

Rose Kim, "Board Eyes Emphasis on American Values," *Newsday*. June 23, 1994.

Jeff Simmons, "Cortines vows to stop board's 'America best' plan," *New York Post*. June 22, 1994.

T.M. Mader, "Lake Leader: Who wouldn't like policy," *Daily Commercial*. March 15, 1994.

Larry Rohter, "Battle Over Patriotism Curriculum," *New York Times*. March 15, 1994.

Rick Badie, "Teachers union plans to oppose Hart proposal," *Orlando Sentinel*. March 20, 1994.

Patrick Buchanan, "The cultural war in Lake County," *New York Post*. March 20, 1994.

Dick Sheridan, "Ebonics KOd in District 24," *Daily News*. January 27, 1997.

Paul Toomey, "Board 24 Votes Down Ebonics, Okays Money For Immigrants," *Times Newsweekly*. January 30, 1997.

Betty M. Cooney, "School District 24 Takes Strong Stand Against Ebonics Curriculum," *Queens Chronicle*. January 30, 1997.

Anne Kadet, "Ebonics Banned in Local Schools," *Queens Ledger*. January 30, 1997.

"School Dist. 24 V.P. Introduces Resolution Rejecting Ebonics," *Queens Chronicle*. January 23, 1997.

"Black English is declared 2d language," *Daily News*. January 13, 1997.

Cameron Stewart, "Words of Warning," *The Australian*. February 22, 1997.

"When Bigots Roar," *Ridgewood Ledger*. January 6, 2000.

Anne Kadet, "Do Illegal Immigrants Deserve an Education?" *Glendale Register*. January 30, 1997.

Paul Toomey, "Board Member Riled At Lack Of English," *Times Newsweekly*. December 21, 1995.

Paul Toomey, "Book Ban Beat By Board At District 24 Meeting," *Times Newsweekly*. February 2, 1995.

M. Paul Jackson, "Resolutions Met With Opposition At SB 24 Meeting," *Glendale Register*. February 9, 1995.

"Borzellieri on ABC's '20/20,'" *Queens Ledger*. December 14, 1995.

Joseph Hosey, "School Bd. Member On 20/20: 'Aliens Have Taken Over,'" *Queens Tribune*. December 14, 1995.

Lisa Gelhaus, "Bilingual Funds Get Okay Despite Protest," *Queens Ledger*. July 14, 1994.

Patricia Mangan, "Bi-lingual ed report stirs furor," *Daily News*. October 21, 1994.
Sam Dillon, "Report Faults Bilingual Education in New York," *New York Times*. October 20, 1994.
Leonard Klie, "Bilingual Ed Grant Attacked By Borzellieri," *Times Newsweekly*. July 14, 1994.
Katti Gray, "Beyond the Semantics," *Newsday*. January 13, 1997.
Liga Eglite, "Board Votes To Support Boy Scouts," *Queens Ledger*. December 21, 2000.
Rob MacKay, "School Board Supports Boy Scouts," *Times Newsweekly*. December 21, 2000.
Hector Flores, "School Board Takes On Chancellor Over Boy Scouts," *Queens Ledger*. December 14, 2000.
Carl Campanile, "Levy recruits gay & lesbian teachers," *New York Post*. August 18, 2000.
Maria Alvarez and Susan Edelman, "Furor over bid to gag teachers on sex lives," *New York Post*. May 13, 1998.
Gary McLendon, "School Board Votes Down Controversial Ban On Words," *Queens Tribune*. May 1-7, 1998.
Heather Boerner. "Teachers strike out at union endorsements," *New York Blade News*. February 12, 1999.
Rosalia Ferraro. "Crew Given an 'F' on Gay Issues," *Newsday*. March 12, 1998.
Katie Szymanski. "Battle brews at P.S. 199," *New York Blade News*. February 27, 1998.
"Homophobes Attack QLGPC Co-chair Again," *QLGPC Newsletter*. November 1997.
Harvey Chasser. "Daniel Dromm on the Offensive: A Message for All," *QLGPC Newsletter*. November 1997.
Ann Marie Mooney. "Teacher Dromm Defends His Right," *Queens Ledger*. January 29, 1998.
Daniel P. Dromm. "Open Gay District 24 Teacher Speaks Out" (letter), *Queens Ledger*. October 30, 1997.
Daniel Dromm. "Why I'm An Out Gay Teacher," *Queens Courier*. July 7, 1999.
Angeline Acain. "Daniel Dromm, A Prince in Queer Queens," *ripemag.com*. March 27, 2001.
Andrea Bernstein. "Feggeddaboudit, Mr. Chips," *New York*. November 6, 1995.

John Toscano. "CSB24…Rainbow Fight Lives On," *Queens Gazette*. May 27, 1993.

Patricia Mangan. "Anti-gay comment by school adviser gains supporters," *Daily News*. June 10, 1994.

Linda Wilson. "Despite Need For Sex Education, Pupils Too Young For AIDS Class," *Queens Gazette*. April 18, 1996.

Paul Toomey. "School District 24 Members Ban Sex Topics; Views Clash At Meeting," *Times Newsweekly*. February 15, 1996.

Sarah Kershaw and Alexandra Poolos. "District Is Divided Over 'Big Four' Ban," *Newsday*. February 14, 1996.

Robert Polner. "The Four Forbidden Words," *Newsday*. February 5, 1996.

M. Paul Jackson. "Board Rejects New Curriculum Proposal at Meeting," *Queens Ledger*. July 13, 1995.

Patricia Mangan. "AIDS course ripped," *Daily News*. January 20, 1995.

Brian Winzeworth. "Jury Still Out On HIV/AIDS Guide Curriculum In Dist 24," *Queens Gazette*. July 13, 1995.

Betty M. Cooney. "C.S.D. #24 To Examine HIV/AIDS Curriculum," *Queens Chronicle*. July 6, 1995.

John Toscano. "Borzellieri Adamant In Stance Against Sex Ed Curriculum," *Queens Gazette*. July 15, 1995.

Paul Toomey. "Crowley Re-elected President of CSB 24," *Times Newsweekly*. June 29, 1995.

Betty M. Cooney. "C.S.B. 24 Blasted For No Vote; New Vote Accepts Federal Aide," *Queens Chronicle*. September 15, 1994.

John Toscano. "Second Time Around, CSB 24 Votes For Fed $," *Queens Gazette*. September 22, 1994.

Linda Ocasio. "20M in ed aid runs into snag," *Daily News*. August 31, 1994.

Shonna Keogan. "School Board Rejects Millions In 'Liberal' Funding," *Queens Tribune*. September 8, 1994.

Miguel Garcilazo, Dick Sheridan and Corey Siemaszko. "Scoutmaster's arrest leaves many baffled," *Daily News*. June 23, 1997.

Dan Havlik. "Murder Charge Against Corona Youth Leader Jolts Western Queens," *Queens Chronicle*. June 26, 1997.

"Unfortunate Incident Mars Scouts," *Queens Ledger*. June 26, 1997.

Anne Kadet and M. Paul Jackson. "School Board member Confesses to Murder," *Queens Ledger*. June 26, 1997.

Jeremy Olshan. "Buckley Resigns from Board 24," *Queens Tribune*. June 26, 1997.

Print Media Sources

Betty M. Cooney. "C.S.B. 24 Member Resigns Seat After Being Indicted For Murder," *Queens Chronicle*. October 17, 1997.
John Toscano. "Borzellieri Leads All Vote-getters In Reelection To SB 24," *Queens Gazette*. June 6, 1996.
David Oats. "Asians & Conservatives Gain On School Boards," *Queens Tribune*. June 6, 1996.
M. Paul Jackson. "School Board Conservative Wins First Place on Board 24," *Queens Ledger*. May 30, 1996.
"It's Borzellieri," *Queens Ledger*. May 30, 1996.
Dick Sheridan. "Incumbent tops in ed race," *Daily News*. May 28, 1996.
Robert Polner. "Right Man For Queens School Post," *Newsday*. May 29, 1996.
"School Board 24 Elections," *Queens Ledger*. May 2, 1996.
Ron Sinacori. "The Writing on the Chalkboard," *Queens Ledger*. May 9, 1996.
M. Paul Jackson. "Controversial School Board Gears Up for Coming Election," *Glendale Register*. May 2, 1996.
"About the District 24 School Board Elections…," *Queens Ledger*. May 30, 1996.
Paul Toomey. "Bd 24 Candidates Make Their Pitch," *Times Newsweekly*. March 14, 1996.
"Mr. Whitebread," *Newsday*. May 21, 1994.
Billy Tashman. "Stalag 24," *Village Voice*. May 24, 1994.
Rose Kim. "Slamming Multicultural Books," *Newsday*. May 17, 1996.
Paul Toomey. "Book Ban Beat By Board At District 24 Meeting," *Times Newsweekly*. February 2, 1995.
"What's the Resolution?" *Jackson Heights News*. February 2, 1995.
"The Liberal Lynching of Frank Borzellieri," *Times Newsweekly*. May 26, 1994.
Michelle Pinto. "Here's One For The Books," *Queens Chronicle*. June 2, 1994.
Luis Francia. "Narrow-minded school board must face diversity," *Daily News*. March 11, 1994.
Lisa Gelhaus. "Bashing Busts Borzellieri's Book Ban," *Long Island City Journal*. May 26, 1994.
"School book critic's battle angers parents," *Daily News*. May 25, 1994.
"Alienation," *Daily News*. May 19, 1994.
Ernie Naspretto. "My Views On Borzellieri's Views," *Queens Chronicle*. May 26, 1994.

"Schools win OK to pick own books," *Daily News*. February 15, 1995.

Robert Trotta. "Community School Board 24 Meeting Ends In A Walkout," *Times Newsweekly*. September 6, 1994.

Brian Winzeworth. "Borzellieri Casts 'No' Vote To $34,000 In Grants," *Queens Gazette*. July 21, 1994.

Betty M. Cooney. "Locals Express Shock & Dismay Over Borzellieri's Bias Statements," *Queens Chronicle*. May 19, 1994.

"The Week," *National Review*. July 10, 1995.

Frank Borzellieri. "Multicultural Schools" (Letter), *National Review*. August 14, 1995.

John Toscano. "Borzellieri, Foes Trade Censorship Charges," *Queens Gazette*. June 2, 1994.

Margaret Ramirez. "Ebonics Allies Make NY Push," *Newsday*. February 8, 1997.

Rose Kim. "Controversy Booked Into District 24," *Newsday*. March 10, 1994.

Audra Delgaudio. "School Board 24 Violating U.S. Constitution By Accepting Grant," *Queens Gazette*. April 11, 1996.

Paul Toomey. "School Board 24 Member Questions Grant Money And Teachers Conference Expenses," *Times Newsweekly*. April 11, 1996.

Marcia Gelbart. "Multiculturalism Is 'Anti-American,'" *Queens Tribune*. March 10, 1994.

Robert Trotta. "New CSB 24 member Attacks Teachings," *Times Newsweekly*. June 10, 1993.

Bill Mitchell. "Multicultural Ed Foe Continues His Fight," *Times Newsweekly*. April 14, 1994.

Marcia Gelbart. "Angry Community Blasts School Board Member," *Queens Tribune*. May 24, 1994.

Lisa Gelhaus. "'Multiculturalism' Incites Debate," *Queens Ledger*. March 10, 1994.

Jeff Simmons. "Queens man on rampage to ban books on diversity," *New York Post*. May 16, 1994.

Michelle Pinto. "More Book Banning Bunk," *Queens Chronicle*. May 19, 1994.

Paul Toomey. "Parents Honored For Help With Asbestos," *Times Newsweekly*. May 25, 1995.

John Toscano. "Bashed On Book Burning, He Bites Back," *Queens Gazette*. May 26, 1994.

"An 'F' For Conduct," *Queens Tribune*. May 26, 1994.

Print Media Sources

Paul Toomey. "CSB 24 Member Hit With Committees Ban," *Times Newsweekly*. May 26, 1994.
Jeff Simmons. "School-board member: Textbooks that aren't Eurocentric are trash," *New York Post*. March 11, 1994.
Rose Kim. "The Right Guff," *Newsday*. July 4, 1994.
Betty M. Cooney. "Borzellieri Named Conservative man Of The Year By Alliance," *Queens Chronicle*. April 6, 1995.
Sam Dillon. "Tension on Queens School Board That Fought Fernandez," *New York Times*. February 19, 1994.
"Two Standards at School Board," *Queens Ledger*. June 9, 1994.
Rose Kim. "Bending the Board's By-Laws," *Newsday*. June 5, 1994.
Catherine Knett. "Letters," *Times Newsweekly*. June 23, 1994.
Marcia Gelbart. "Book Banning Board Member Called Racist By Parents," *Queens Tribune*. May 19, 1994.
Rose Kim. "All-American Book Battle," *Newsday*. May 20, 1994.
Rose Kim. "Board Member Slammed," *Newsday*. May 18, 1994.
Gina Parker. "140 Teachers To Be Tenured Held Captive by School Board 24," *Queens Ledger*. October 2, 1997.
Linda Ocasio. "Board member hit on school book ban bid," *Daily News*. May 18, 1994.
Sarah Kershaw. "One-Man Crusade," *Newsday*. December 13, 1998.

Index

A

"A+ For Kids", 65
Allenby, Ted, 19
Alvarado, Miguel, 100
"America's British Culture", 40, 82
Anastasiou, George, 155
Angelou, Maya, 12, 31
Auster, Lawrence, 55

B

Bagley, Ed, 11
Ballou, Thomas, 55
Barron, Charles, 120
"A Basic History of the United States", 82
"The Battle of Lexington and Concord", 82
Bey, Richard, 65, 66
Birbiglia, Jack, 140, 141, 147, 148
Boone, Daniel, 98
Boy Scouts of America, 142, 160, 161, 162, 163, 164, 171
Bradford, M.E., 84
Bridges, Linda, 67
Brookhiser, Richard, 67
Buchanan, Patrick, 51, 52, 72, 76
Buckley, Perry, 24, 25, 26, 29, 36, 40, 42, 120, 177
Buckley, William, F., 25, 54
Bunker, Archie, 116

C

"Calypso Alphabet", 32
Carlin, George, 82
Carson, Clarence, 82
Center for Equal Opportunity, 102
Cermeli, Robert, 155, 163, 177
Chan, Carolyn, 137
Chan, Louisa, 55, 80, 95, 98, 104, 106, 126, 134, 136, 137, 138, 152, 155, 156, 163, 176
Chavez, Linda, 51, 102
Chavis, Ben, 48
"A Children's Companion Guide to America's History: History and Government", 83
Christian Coalition, 50
"Christianity and the Constitution: The Faith of Our Founding Fathers", 83
Civiello, Mary, 85
Cleopatra, 17
Clinton, Bill, 31
"Columbus & Cortez, Conquerors for Christ", 83
Columbus, Christopher, 5, 12, 32, 34, 37, 50, 84
Cook, Toni, 118
Cooney, Betty, 134
Copernicus, Nicholas, 8
Cortines, Ramon, 44, 50, 77, 78, 87, 88, 89, 103, 177
Crew, Rudy, 7, 26, 118, 149
Crowley, Joseph, 60

Crowley, Mary, 28, 29, 30, 46, 47, 48, 53, 54, 55, 56, 60, 61, 62, 63, 77, 78, 79, 85, 88, 89, 91, 92, 95, 97, 98, 105, 133, 155, 177

Cummins, Mary, 6, 9, 10, 11, 19, 20, 22, 24, 27, 28, 42, 43, 44, 53, 75, 76, 78, 86, 87, 92, 93, 94, 95, 97, 98, 106, 122, 123, 124, 125, 127, 128, 129, 133, 140, 143, 166, 177

D

"Daddy's Roommate", 9
"Daniel Boone, Man of the Forests", 83, 96
Davis, Ron, 153
Diamond, Jay, 21, 22, 24, 35, 42, 126
"A Documentary History of Religion in America Since 1865", 83
"A Documentary History of Religion in America to the Civil War", 83
Dromm, Daniel, 48, 138, 139, 140, 141, 142, 143, 144, 146, 147, 148, 149, 150, 151, 152, 153, 155, 156, 157, 160, 162, 177
Duane, Tom, 152
Duke, David, 40
Dunleavy, Steve, 158

E

Earth Day, 68
Edelman, Marian Wright, 31
Eidsmoe, John, 83
Emanuel, Louise, 25
Ethical Culture Society of Queens, 149, 150
"Exploring American History", 85

F

Family Defense Council, 147
Farrakhan, Louis, 48
Faulk, Iris, 26
Feeney, Tom, 65, 74
Fernandez, Joseph, 9, 159
Feuer, Karen, 161
Fiber, Gail, 102
Focus on the Family, 144, 145
"Forked Tongue: The Politics of Bilingual Education", 102
"Founding Fathers: Brief Lives of the Framers of the United States Constitution", 83, 84
Francia, Luis, 29
Frank, Barney, 14
Franklin, Benjamin, 31
Free Teens, 130
Freeman, Douglas Southall, 84

G

Gambino, Elizabeth, 55, 80, 86, 87, 88, 90, 91, 92, 93, 95, 96, 97, 98, 104, 105, 176

Garkowski, John, 10, 11, 12, 28, 30, 45, 46, 57, 87, 89, 90, 93, 94, 95, 97, 121, 124, 125, 128, 129, 133, 153, 166, 177
Garvey, Marcus, 19
Gaustad, Edwin S., 83
Gay Activist Alliance, 142, 143
Geremia, Sharon, 155
"Geronimo", 18, 25
Giuliani, Rudolph, 4, 33, 36, 37, 161
Gizzi, John, 43
Glendale Taxpayers Association, 168
"Gloria Goes Gay Pride", 9
Goals 2000, 12
"The Godfather", 38
Gonzalez, Josue, 101
Grant, Bob, 21, 22, 35, 42, 57, 58, 75, 76
Green, Mark, 59
Greene, Carol, 83
Guevera, Che, 75

H

"Haitian Days", 32
Haley, Alex, 172
Hanson, Jane, 85
Harris, Reggie, 36
Hart, Pat, 70
"Heather Has Two Mommies", 9, 44, 49
Helms, Jesse, 39, 50
Hevesi, Alan, 48, 51, 53, 54, 156, 177

"A History of Christianity in the United States and Canada", 84
Ho Chi Minh, 19
Human Events, 9, 43, 164
Hurwitz, Howard, 139, 140, 147, 148, 149, 150, 151

I

"I Hate English", 32, 48, 64
Innis, Roy, 22, 23, 27, 42
"Inside American Education", 18, 20, 45, 51, 54

J

Jackson, Jesse, 14, 30, 43, 50
"Jambo Means Hello", 32, 127
Jamerson, Doug, 71, 72
"Jaws", 18
Jefferson, Thomas, 7, 31
Jeffries, Leonard, 18, 23, 48, 50, 51, 63
Johnson, Lyndon, 35
Johnson, Neil, 82

K

Katz, Melinda, 54
Kennedy, John, 35
Kennedy, Robert, 35
Kershaw, Sarah, 128
Kim, Rose, 33, 60
King, Martin Luther, 5, 32, 34, 35, 36, 37, 42, 46, 53, 54, 58, 67, 76, 143, 150, 151
Kinsey, Alfred, 144, 145, 146

Kirk, Russell, 40, 41, 82
Knett, Catherine, 63
Koch, Ed, 4, 40, 42
"Korean Cinderella", 32
Ku Klux Klan, 18, 53
Kudlow, Larry, 67
Kwanzaa, 68

L
"La Fiesta Del Abecedano", 32
La Raza, 169
Lake, Ricki, 165
LaRock, J.D., 7
LaSala, Jake, 55, 80, 87, 95, 125, 176
"The Last Angry Principal", 147
Lazaro, Mary, 137, 155
Lear, Norman, 48
Lebron, Michael, 34, 35
Ledee, Carlos, 104, 105, 106, 110
Lesbian and Gay Teachers Association, 141
Levine, Ellen, 48
Levy, Harold, 159, 160, 161, 164, 177
"The Light and the Glory for Children: Discovering God's Plan for America from Christopher Columbus to George Washington", 84
Lincoln, Abraham, 136
London, Herbert, 23, 27, 42, 50

Longfellow, Henry Wadsworth, 84, 89
Lowry, Rich, 43, 67
Luciano, Felipe, 40, 42
Lugo, Enrique, 108, 109, 110

M
Madison, Dolly, 66
Mahlke, Wayne, 143, 157, 158, 159, 162, 177
Malcolm X, 12
Manuel, David, 84
Mao Tse-tung, 94
Marlowe, Catherine, 95, 155, 158, 170, 171, 172, 176
Marshall, Helen, 54, 55
Marshall, Peter, 84
Marx Brothers, 54
Marx, Karl, 75, 132
Masi, Kathy, 28, 30, 120, 134, 136, 155, 176
Mazer, Bill, 53
McCaffrey, Walter, 152
McHale, Linda, 94
Megan's Law, 7
Millard, Catherine, 83
Monteith, Stanley, 146
Moore, Michael, 14
Morgenstern, Gloria, 156
Morris, Geoffrey, 43
Morrison, Toni, 31, 36
Moses, 17
Muhammed, Kaleed, 61
Mullins, Keith, 72

N
NAACP, 30, 48, 52, 56, 65, 74
Naspretto, Ernest, 61
National Association for Bilingual Education, 101, 104
National Coalition Against Censorship, 59
National Endowment for the Arts, 39, 50
National Review, 24, 43, 44, 45, 51, 54, 66, 67, 90
New York Blade, 151
New York Civil Liberties Union, 36, 48, 81
New York Magazine, 140
Noll, Mark A., 84
Noviello, James, 26, 27

O
O'Donnell, Rosie, 157
O'Sullivan, John, 24, 51, 67

P
"Palo Mayombe", 73
Parker, Rosemary, 137
"Path to National Suicide", 55
"Paul Revere's Ride", 84
Pearson, Judy, 71
Picicci, Susan, 137
Pizzo, Jeanne, 125
Porter, Rosalie Pedalino, 102

Q
Queens Lesbian and Gay Pride Committee, 48

Quinn, Joseph, 19, 91, 93, 105, 110, 148, 149

R
Reagan, Ronald, 35
Reed, Ralph, 50
Reisman, Judith, 144, 145
Ricardo, David, 16
Richardson, Charles, 31
"Ring My Bell", 87
Ringling Brothers, 53
Ripe Magazine, 142
Rivera, Geraldo, 4, 65, 74
Roe vs. Wade, 154
Rogers, Fred, 168
Rosenthal, Abe, 72

S
Sabini, John, 152
Saccoccio, August, 150
Sanchez, Walter, 162, 163, 171, 172
Sansivieri, Linda, 21, 22, 24, 27, 47, 52, 53, 76, 86, 87, 92, 93, 94, 125, 134, 155, 176
Santeria, 73
Santiago, Isaura, 104
Satan, 167
Savonarola, 29
Schwartz, Richard, 37
"Sexual Behavior in the Human Male", 144, 145
Sharpton, Al, 158
Sherman, William Tecumseh, 21
Sherr, Lynn, 106

Siegel, Norman, 48, 81
Sliwa, Curtis, 87
Smith, Adam, 75
Sobol, Thomas, 18, 50
Socrates, 68
"Sombrero of Luis Luceo", 32
Sowell, Thomas, 4, 10, 18, 20, 45, 51, 54, 101, 130, 132, 136
Stalin, Joseph, 22, 34
Stavisky, Leonard, 126, 127
Steele, Shelby, 118
"Street Talk", 39, 42
Szymanski, Katie, 151

T

Ten Commandments, 76
"Tikki Tikki Tembo", 32
Thomson, Terri, 159, 160
Toomey, Paul, 136
"A Treasury of Children's Literature", 84

U

Unger, Bob, 13, 31
United Federation of Teachers, 80, 91, 153

V

Van Bramer, Jimmy, 162
Vella, Marie, 163
Village Voice, 62, 90

W

"Washington", 84
Washington, George, 7, 31, 75, 84
Weiner, Howard, 124, 126
Williams, Polly, 43
Witkowski, Dorothy, 137
"Wizard of Oz", 168

Y

"Young Martin's Promise", 59, 172

Other Books by Frank Borzellieri

The Unspoken Truth: Race, Culture and Other Taboos
$22.95 postage paid

Don't Take It Personally: Race, Immigration, Crime and Other Heresies
$24.95 postage paid

Order both books for only $40 postage paid! (Save $8)

To order other books by Frank Borzellieri, visit:

www.culturalstudiespress.com

Or send payment to:

Cultural Studies Press
P.O. Box 1492
New York, New York 10163

About the Author

Frank Borzellieri is adjunct professor of journalism and media writing at St. John's University in New York City. He is the author of five books on politics, social commentary, and history and has written hundreds of newspaper articles published in a variety of journals including *Newsday*, *USA Today*, the *New York Daily News*, and many others.

He has been profiled in many major newspapers and magazines including the *New York Times*, *Washington Times*, *New York Post*, and the *Village Voice*.

Frank Borzellieri has appeared on many television programs including ABC's 20/20, the Ricki Lake Show, Geraldo Rivera, Fox Sunday Morning, Good Morning America, Leeza Gibbons and scores of radio shows including Sean Hannity, Alan Colmes, Curtis Sliwa, and Bob Grant.

Cultural Studies Press